First World War
and Army of Occupation
War Diary
France, Belgium and Germany

35 DIVISION
106 Infantry Brigade
Royal Scots (Lothian Regiment)
17th Battalion
31 January 1916 - 22 April 1919

WO95/2490/3

The Naval & Military Press Ltd
www.nmarchive.com
Published in association with The National Archives

Published by

The Naval & Military Press Ltd

Unit 10 Ridgewood Industrial Park,

Uckfield, East Sussex,

TN22 5QE England

Tel: +44 (0) 1825 749494

www.naval-military-press.com

www.nmarchive.com

This diary has been reprinted in facsimile from the original. Any imperfections are inevitably reproduced and the quality may fall short of modern type and cartographic standards.

© **Crown Copyright**
Images reproduced by permission of The National Archives, London, England, 2015.

Contents

Document type	Place/Title	Date From	Date To
Heading	WO95/2490/3		
Heading	35th Division 106th Infy Bde 17th Bn Royal Scots Jan 1916-Apr 1919		
Heading	17th Royal Scots 35th Div Vol 1 Feb 16 Ap 19		
Miscellaneous	The Officer i/c A. G.s Office At The Base.	29/02/1916	29/02/1916
War Diary	Perham Downs Southampton	31/01/1916	31/01/1916
War Diary	Havre	01/02/1916	02/02/1916
War Diary	Wardrecques	03/02/1916	09/02/1916
War Diary	Boeseghem	10/02/1916	18/02/1916
War Diary	Merville	19/02/1916	19/02/1916
War Diary	Arrewage	20/02/1916	20/02/1916
War Diary	Trenches	21/02/1916	26/02/1916
War Diary	Arrewage	27/02/1916	29/02/1916
Heading	17 R Scots Vol 2		
War Diary	Arrewage	01/03/1916	05/03/1916
War Diary	La Gorgue	06/03/1916	06/03/1916
War Diary	Trenches	07/03/1916	11/03/1916
War Diary	Riezbailleul	12/03/1916	13/03/1916
War Diary	Pacaud	14/03/1916	18/03/1916
War Diary	Cornet Malo	19/03/1916	26/03/1916
War Diary	Estaires	27/03/1916	27/03/1916
War Diary	Trenches	28/03/1916	31/03/1916
War Diary	Rouse de Bout	01/04/1916	16/04/1916
War Diary	Croix Barbee	18/04/1916	28/04/1916
War Diary	Croix Marmuse	06/05/1916	06/05/1916
War Diary	Ferme Du Bois	07/05/1916	10/05/1916
War Diary	Le Touret	15/05/1916	15/05/1916
War Diary	Farme Du Bois	16/05/1916	18/05/1916
War Diary	Letouret	19/05/1916	19/05/1916
War Diary	Leslobes	22/05/1916	22/05/1916
War Diary	Festubert	28/05/1916	31/05/1916
War Diary	Trenches	01/06/1916	01/06/1916
War Diary	Festubert Village Line	02/06/1916	02/06/1916
War Diary	Trenches	05/06/1916	11/06/1916
War Diary	Leslobes	12/06/1916	12/06/1916
War Diary	Mont Bernard Chon	16/06/1916	16/06/1916
War Diary	Near Busnes	17/06/1916	17/06/1916
War Diary	Oblinghem	18/06/1916	30/06/1916
Heading	106th Bde. 35th Div. 17th Battalion The Royal Scots to 31st July 1916 Report on Operations 29/30th with G.S. Diary.		
War Diary	50.a.R.S	02/07/1916	30/07/1916
Heading	106th Brigade 35th Division. 17th Battalion The Royal Scots August 1916		
War Diary	Monlancourt	01/08/1916	01/08/1916
War Diary	Saisseval	05/08/1916	28/08/1916
War Diary	Bernaville	30/08/1916	30/08/1916
War Diary	Sus St. Leger	31/08/1916	31/08/1916
War Diary		01/09/1916	30/09/1916
War Diary	Arras	01/10/1916	03/11/1916

War Diary	Trenches	04/11/1916	09/11/1916
War Diary	Arras	10/11/1916	15/11/1916
War Diary	Trenches	16/11/1916	22/11/1916
War Diary	Arras	23/11/1916	28/11/1916
War Diary	Trenches	29/11/1916	01/12/1916
War Diary	Arras	02/12/1916	02/12/1916
War Diary	Dainville	02/12/1916	02/12/1916
War Diary	Gouy-En-Ternois	03/12/1916	07/12/1916
War Diary	Ternas	08/12/1916	29/12/1916
War Diary	Arras	29/12/1916	03/02/1917
War Diary	Gouy. En. Ternois	06/02/1917	07/02/1917
War Diary	Vignacourt.	08/02/1917	19/02/1917
War Diary	Marcel Cave	22/02/1917	26/02/1917
War Diary	Rosieres	01/03/1917	02/03/1917
War Diary	Trenches	03/03/1917	09/03/1917
War Diary	Rosieres	09/03/1917	09/03/1917
War Diary	Trenches	10/03/1917	14/03/1917
War Diary	Trenches Rosieres	14/03/1917	15/03/1917
War Diary	Camp Des Ballons	16/03/1917	17/03/1917
War Diary	Rosieres	17/03/1917	18/03/1917
War Diary	Trenches	18/03/1917	18/03/1917
War Diary	Hallu Rouvroy	19/03/1917	19/03/1917
War Diary	Rosieres	20/03/1917	23/03/1917
War Diary	Licourt	29/03/1917	30/03/1917
War Diary	Y and Croix-Molignaux	30/03/1917	30/03/1917
War Diary	Croix-Molic-Naux	01/04/1917	08/04/1917
War Diary	Monchy Lagache	09/04/1917	09/04/1917
War Diary	Soyecourt	10/04/1917	12/04/1917
War Diary	Front Line Near Berthaucourt	12/04/1917	16/04/1917
War Diary	Vermand	16/04/1917	20/04/1917
War Diary	Front Line Near Berthaucourt	20/04/1917	23/04/1917
War Diary	Villeveque	23/04/1917	29/04/1917
War Diary	Maissemy	30/04/1917	30/04/1917
Diagram etc	Map 1/20,000 Sheet 62 B S.W.		
War Diary	Maissemy	01/05/1917	03/05/1917
War Diary	Front Line N.W. of Fresnoy	03/05/1917	08/05/1917
War Diary	Villevecque	08/05/1917	12/05/1917
War Diary	Villecholles	14/05/1917	18/05/1917
War Diary	Tertry	18/05/1917	18/05/1917
War Diary	Peronne	19/05/1917	20/05/1917
War Diary	Templeux-La-Fosse	21/05/1917	26/05/1917
War Diary	Villers-Guislain (front Line Near)	26/05/1917	26/05/1917
War Diary	Front Line Near Villers-Guislans	01/06/1917	02/06/1917
War Diary	Aizicourt-Le. Bas	03/06/1917	04/06/1917
War Diary	Heudicourt	10/06/1917	17/06/1917
War Diary	Front Line Trenches Near Gonnelieu.	18/06/1917	26/06/1917
War Diary	Aizicourt Le Bas	27/06/1917	30/06/1917
Diagram etc	Ref. Map 1/20,000 Sheet 57c S E		
War Diary	Templeux-La Fosse	01/07/1917	01/07/1917
War Diary	Longavesnes	02/07/1917	06/07/1917
War Diary	Lempire	06/07/1917	14/07/1917
War Diary	Front Line	14/07/1917	14/07/1917
War Diary	Trenches C2 Sub-Sector	14/07/1917	31/07/1917
War Diary	Lempire	01/08/1917	01/09/1917
War Diary	Templeux-La-Fosse	02/09/1917	05/09/1917
War Diary	Epehy	06/09/1917	16/09/1917

War Diary	Templeux-La Fosse	18/09/1917	26/09/1917
War Diary	St. Emilie	26/09/1917	01/10/1917
War Diary	Templeux La Fosse	02/10/1917	02/10/1917
War Diary		03/10/1917	03/10/1917
War Diary	Peronne	04/10/1917	04/10/1917
War Diary	Duisans	05/10/1917	13/10/1917
War Diary	Hogenhill	14/10/1917	16/10/1917
War Diary	Proven	17/10/1917	17/10/1917
War Diary	Trenches	18/10/1917	29/10/1917
War Diary	Proven	30/10/1917	30/10/1917
War Diary	Hothuli St Forest	01/11/1917	30/11/1917
War Diary	Near Pilkem	01/12/1917	01/12/1917
War Diary	Near Elverdinghe	02/12/1917	05/12/1917
War Diary	Near Woesten	05/12/1917	11/12/1917
War Diary	Near Watou	11/12/1917	31/12/1917
War Diary	Near Ypres	21/12/1917	27/12/1917
War Diary	Near Watou	27/12/1917	27/12/1917
War Diary	Front Line Near Poelcapelle	25/01/1918	29/01/1918
War Diary	Wieltje	29/01/1918	31/01/1918
War Diary	Near Watou	01/01/1918	08/01/1918
War Diary	Near Ypres	08/01/1918	16/01/1918
War Diary	Elverdinghe	16/01/1918	21/01/1918
War Diary	St. Julien	21/01/1918	25/01/1918
War Diary	Near Wieltje	01/02/1918	04/02/1918
War Diary	Near Poelcapelle	04/02/1918	08/02/1918
War Diary	Elverdinghe	08/02/1918	16/02/1918
War Diary	Langemarck	16/02/1918	18/02/1918
War Diary	Houthoul St Forest	18/02/1918	22/02/1918
War Diary	Near Pilkem	22/02/1918	28/02/1918
Heading	106th Inf. Bde. 35th Div. 17th Battn. The Royal Scots. March 1918		
War Diary	Elverdinghe	01/03/1918	07/03/1918
War Diary	Houthoul St Forest	07/03/1918	09/03/1918
War Diary	Near Poperinghe	09/03/1918	22/03/1918
War Diary	Proven	23/03/1918	23/03/1918
War Diary	Heilly	23/03/1918	23/03/1918
War Diary	Bray-Sur. Somme	23/03/1918	24/03/1918
War Diary	Maricourt	24/03/1918	24/03/1918
War Diary	Near Hem	24/03/1918	24/03/1918
War Diary	Curlu	24/03/1918	25/03/1918
War Diary	Maricourt	25/03/1918	25/03/1918
War Diary	Bray-Sur-Somme.	26/03/1918	26/03/1918
War Diary	Morlancourt	26/03/1918	26/03/1918
War Diary	Buire. Sur. L'Ancre	26/03/1918	26/03/1918
War Diary	Lavieville	27/03/1918	27/03/1918
War Diary	Near Dernancourt	27/03/1918	29/03/1918
War Diary	Near Buire-Sur. L'Ancre	29/03/1918	30/03/1918
War Diary	Heilly	30/03/1918	04/04/1918
War Diary	Baizieux	05/04/1918	05/04/1918
War Diary	Martinsart	06/04/1918	11/04/1918
War Diary	Hedauville	11/04/1918	14/04/1918
War Diary	Bouzincourt	14/04/1918	20/04/1918
War Diary	Hedauville	20/04/1918	23/04/1918
War Diary	Martinsart	23/04/1918	27/04/1918
War Diary	Hedauville	29/04/1918	29/04/1918
War Diary	Rubempre	30/04/1918	30/04/1918

War Diary	Rubempre Near Warloy	01/05/1918	11/05/1918
War Diary	Rubempre.	13/05/1918	19/05/1918
War Diary	In Line	21/05/1918	29/05/1918
War Diary	Martinss Art	01/06/1918	16/06/1918
War Diary	Warloy Raincheval	17/06/1918	30/06/1918
War Diary	Doullens	01/07/1918	01/07/1918
War Diary	Le Nieppe	02/07/1918	02/07/1918
War Diary	Zermezeele	03/07/1918	03/07/1918
War Diary	St. Laurent	05/07/1918	10/07/1918
War Diary	Trenches	10/07/1918	31/07/1918
War Diary	Mont Vidaigne	01/08/1918	02/08/1918
War Diary	Boeschepe	03/08/1918	04/08/1918
War Diary	Mont Vidaigne	05/08/1918	09/08/1918
War Diary	Eecke	10/08/1918	17/08/1918
War Diary	Lewast	18/08/1918	23/08/1918
War Diary	Eecke	24/08/1918	31/08/1918
War Diary	Steenvoorde	01/09/1918	02/09/1918
War Diary	Trenches	03/09/1918	07/09/1918
War Diary	Erie Camp	12/09/1918	13/09/1918
War Diary	Trenches	16/09/1918	30/09/1918
Miscellaneous	17th (S) Bn. The Royal Scots. Report on operations engaged in from 25th September 1918 until 1st October 1918	25/09/1918	25/09/1918
Operation(al) Order(s)	17th The Royal Scots. Operations Order No. 104	26/09/1918	26/09/1918
War Diary	Belgian Battery Corner	03/10/1918	04/10/1918
War Diary	V.24.a.	07/10/1918	07/10/1918
War Diary	V.20.b.	11/10/1918	31/10/1918
War Diary	V.20.b.	21/10/1918	31/10/1918
Miscellaneous	17th. (S). Bn. The Royal Scots. Report On Operations engaged in by the Battalion from 13th. Oct. to 21st. Oct. 1918	13/10/1918	13/10/1918
War Diary	Evangelice Boom	31/10/1918	04/11/1918
War Diary	Courtrai	04/11/1918	09/11/1918
War Diary	Ingoyghem	09/11/1918	09/11/1918
War Diary	Mont de la Cruche	10/11/1918	10/11/1918
War Diary	Ten Bergg	11/11/1918	13/11/1918
War Diary	Eticheve	13/11/1918	18/11/1918
War Diary	Ingoyghem	18/11/1918	18/11/1918
War Diary	Staceghem	19/11/1918	27/11/1918
War Diary	Menin	27/11/1918	27/11/1918
War Diary	Ypres	28/11/1918	28/11/1918
War Diary	Terdeghem	29/11/1918	29/11/1918
War Diary	Broxeele	30/11/1918	30/11/1918
War Diary	Moulle	01/12/1918	01/12/1918
War Diary	Broxeele	01/12/1918	31/12/1918
War Diary	Merckeghem	01/01/1919	31/01/1919
War Diary	Calais	01/02/1919	28/02/1919
War Diary	Merckeghem	01/04/1919	22/04/1919

WO 95/24903

35TH DIVISION
106TH INFY BDE

WO 95

17TH BN ROYAL SCOTS
JAN ~~FEB~~ 1916 - APR 1919

17th Royal Scots.
35 Bde
Vol. 1

Feb. '16
Ap. '19

Secret.

The Officer I/c A.G.'s office at the Base.

Herewith War Diary for the month of February.

R.D. Cheales. Lt.Col -
Cmmdg 17th S.Bn Royal Scots

29/2/16.

Army Form C. 2118

17th ROYAL SCOTS.

WAR DIARY
or
INTELLIGENCE SUMMARY

(Erase heading not required.)

Instructions regarding War Diaries and Intelligence Summaries are contained in F. S. Regs., Part II. and the Staff Manual respectively. Title Pages will be prepared in manuscript.

Place	Date	Hour	Summary of Events and Information	Remarks and references to Appendices
PERHAM DOWNS	31st Jan.	8.30 a.m.	Battalion entrained in three portions. Arrived SOUTHAMPTON. Left SOUTHAMPTON in two ships S.S. LYDIA and CONNAUGHT. Roll of Officers attached. Weather fine. Reached HAVRE 10.45 p.m.	Base Post
SOUTHAMPTON				Post
HAVRE	1st Feb.	7.30 a.m.	Disembarked and marched to Rest Camp, 5 miles. Weather fine, cold night	Post
"	2nd "	9 a.m.	Advanced party of 3 Officers and 125 O.R. entrained. Weather fine.	Post
"	"	4 p.m.	Remainder of Battalion entrained. Train left at 8 p.m. map 36A	Post
WARDRECQUES	3rd Feb.	4.30 p.m.	Arrived and detrained and marched to billets at WARDRECQUES, 5 miles. Arrived 7.30 p.m.	Post
"	4th "		Muster parade and inspection of Equipment. Weather changeable.	Post
"	5th "		Battalion Route march, 5 miles. Weather fine and sunny.	Post
"	6th "		C.O. and Adjutant to Machine Gun lectures at WISQES. Weather wet. Coy Commanders and NCOs to HEADQUARTER'S GUARDS DIVISION for instruction.	Post
"	7th "		Company Route Marches. Weather fine.	Post
"	8th "		Company Route Marches. Weather Wet. Cleaning billets. map 36A	Post
BOESEGHEM	9th "	11.30 a.m.	Battalion marched from WARDRECQUES to billets at BOESEGHEM, 6 miles. Weather fine.	Post
"	10th "		Battalion Route March. Weather fine.	Post
"	11th "		Inspected by Field Marshal Viscount KITCHENER. Weather very wet.	Post
"	12th "		Company Route Marches. Weather fine.	Post
"	13th "		Church Parade. Kit inspections etc. Weather changeable.	Post
"	14th "		Company Route Marches. Weather changeable.	Post
"	15th "		Anti-gas demonstration and lecture. Weather changeable.	Post
"	16th "		Lectures by Major Gen. Sir R. HAKING to Officers of 35th Div. Weather changeable.	Post
"	17th "		Cleaning billets preparatory to move.	Post
"	18th "	8.30 a.m.	Marched from BOESEGHEM, map 36A to billets at MERVILLE, map 36A. 10 miles. Very wet.	Post
MERVILLE	19th "	9 a.m.	Marched to new billets at ARREWAGE, map 36A. 2 miles. Weather fine	Post

Army Form C. 2118

1/7th ROYAL SCOTS.
WAR DIARY
or
INTELLIGENCE SUMMARY
(Erase heading not required.)

Instructions regarding War Diaries and Intelligence Summaries are contained in F.S. Regs., Part II. and the Staff Manual respectively. Title Pages will be prepared in manuscript.

Place	Date	Hour	Summary of Events and Information	Remarks and references to Appendices
ARREWAGE	20th Feb.	9 a.m.	Left billets at 9, and marched to VIELLE CHAPELLE (Map BETHUNE combined sheet): then met by guides and taken W Company to 7th R. LANCASTER REGT., X Company to 7th E. LANC. REGT.	
TRENCHES.	21st		Y Company to 7th S. LANG. REGT. Z Company to 7th NORTH LANC. REGT. Headquarters 5, 56th Infy. Bde. X and Z went into trenches with their respective Regts. for instruction. W and Y to their respective Battalion's billets. C.O. and Adjt to 7th E. LANC REGT.	nil nil
"	22nd		X and Z Companies came out of trenches, and W and Y went in.	nil
"	24th		W and Y Companies came out of trenches and X and Z went in.	nil
"	26th		X and Z Companies came out of trenches and W and Y went in.	nil
ARREWAGE	27th	10 a.m.	X and Z Companies marched back to billets at ARREWAGE, Map 36 A	nil
"	28th	"	W and Y Companies marched back to billets at ARREWAGE. Map 36 A	nil
			During the period of instruction, platoons and Sections were given a portion of the line to hold. Men were taken out in front for wiring and patrolling, and Officers and N.C.Os were taught their various duties. During the first part of the time the Wind was West, then it veered to East, and units were warned to expect a gas attack. The last part of the time Snow fell heavily, and there was a sharp frost. There were six casualties, 4 slight wounds, 2 severe, one man	nil
"	29th	10 a.m.	having his arm blown off by a shell from one of our own guns as he was walking along a road while back in billets. A court of Enquiry was held by order of the BRIGADIER 56th BDE. Battalion to the Baths at St VENANT	

35th

17 R Scots

Vol 2

WAR DIARY or INTELLIGENCE SUMMARY

Army Form C. 2118

17th ROYAL SCOTS

Place	Date	Hour	Summary of Events and Information	Remarks and references to Appendices
ARREWAGE	Mar 1st		Battalion sent parties of men to St VENANT for bathing. (Map 36 A)	
"	2nd		Large fatigue parties at the Forest of NIEPPE making ranges. (Map 36A)	
"	3rd		"	
"	4th		Snowstorm which prevented work being carried on at Forest of NIEPPE. (Map 36A) Battalion inspected by Gen. Sir R. HAKING Comdg XI Corps.	
"	5th		Heavy snowstorm again.	
LA GORGUE	6th		Battalion marched to LA GORGUE (Map 36A) about 5 miles, into Billets there.	
TRENCHES	7th		Battalion took over the line of trenches held by 8th N. STAFFORDS, a frontage of about 1500 yards with 3 Keeps, line being the left subsector of the right section of the right Division. running from SIGN POST LANE to MOATED GRANGE (Trench Map 36 S) Relief completed by 8.30 pm.	
"	8th		Quiet day. Trenches very wet from effects of snow. good communication trench.	
"	9th		Heavy bombardment by our guns which drew retaliation from the enemy, their shells falling behind Y Coys lines. Patrols went out to inspect wire. Met no hostile patrols.	
"	10th		Heavy bombardment again, + heavy retaliation from the enemy, which knocked about STILLELOY C.T. and also TILLELOY KEEP. Patrols out at night inspecting wire.	
"	11th		Quiet day, much activity by enemy M.Guns at night during relief of Battalion by 18th H.L.I. Relief completed by 10 p.m. Marched to Billets at RIEZ BAILLEUL. Map Combined Sheet BETHUNE. Total casualties. 7 killed. 6 wounded	

Army Form C. 2118

17th ROYAL SCOTS

WAR DIARY or INTELLIGENCE SUMMARY
(Erase heading not required.)

Instructions regarding War Diaries and Intelligence Summaries are contained in F.S. Regs., Part II. and the Staff Manual respectively. Title Pages will be prepared in manuscript.

Place	Date March	Hour	Summary of Events and Information	Remarks and references to Appendices
TRENCHES	11th		The distribution of the Battn. while in the Trenches was as follows:— on the right Z Coy. 5 officers and 202 r.i.f. on right centre X. Coy. 5 officers, 195 r.i.f. on left centre W Coy. 2½ platoons, 2 officers, 148 r.i.f. on left Y Coy. 4 officers, 205 r.i.f. LAFONE POST 2 officers, 31 r.i.f. W Coy. POMPHOUSE POST 1 officer, 20 r.i.f. STILLELOY KEEP 1 officer, 20 r.i.f. W. Coy. BTN HDQRS. 6 officers, 43 r.i.f. Wet, snowy weather for the first 3 days.	Casualties 6 killed 2 died of wounds 6 wounded
RIEZBAILLEUL	12th		Battalion resting, having Baths.	
"	13th		Remainder of Battalion to the Baths.	
PAÇAUD	14th		Battalion moved to billets at PAÇAUD (Map 36A)	
"	15th		Battalion cleaning Kit, equipment etc. Gas alarm at night, but a false one.	
"	16th		Drill with gas helmets, wiring drill etc.	
"	17th		Route marches by Companies.	
"	18th		" " "	
CORNET MALO	19th		Battalion moved to new Billets at CORNET MALO (Map 36 A)	Draft of 30 men arrived from Base.
"	20th		Battalion in Rest billets.	
"	21st		" " "	
"	22nd		" " "	
"	23rd		" " "	
"	24th		" " "	
"	25th		" " "	

Army Form C. 2118

WAR DIARY or INTELLIGENCE SUMMARY

17th ROYAL SCOTS

(Erase heading not required.)

Instructions regarding War Diaries and Intelligence Summaries are contained in F. S. Regs., Part II. and the Staff Manual respectively. Title Pages will be prepared in manuscript.

Place	Date March	Hour	Summary of Events and Information	Remarks and references to Appendices
CORNET MALO ESTAIRES	26th 27th		Battalion marched to Billets at ESTAIRES. (Map 36 A). Battalion marched to TRENCHES, PETILLON Section, due EAST of LAVENTIE, SOUTH WEST of ARMENTIERES (Map 36). Distribution was as follows — on the right W. Coy, on the right Centre X Coy, on the left centre Y Coy, left Z Coy. Each Coy minus 1 platoon. In BEE and TROU POSTS 2 Sections in each post. 1 platoon from W. Y. Z. Coys in Reserve near Battalion H.Qrs on RUE du BOIS and at TWO TREE FARM. (Trench map 36. S.W.1.) Weather very wet. Relieved 2nd Rifle Brigade. Relief Completed at 10.20 p.m.	Distance between lines varies from 400 to 100 x
TRENCHES	28th		Night of 27th 28th very quiet. During the day enemy shelled our Reserve line between AID POST, V.C. Corner and TWO TREE FARM. Very little M.G or rifle fire during day.	
"	29th		Rifle grenades were thrown into Y and Z Coy lines. 3 men wounded. Retaliated with rifle grenades. Enemy shelled our front line and support posts with shrapnel (whizbangs) no damage done. Patrols went out during night. Weather fine and cold. Wind N.W.	
"	30th		A quiet morning. In the afternoon our Reserve post and Battalion H.Q. heavily shelled by enemy. One Billet occupied by Y Coy burnt to the ground. 2 direct hits on Battalion M.d Q. Patrols active during night, also wiring parties. Fin day.	Total casualties 7 wounded
"	31st		Reserve post again shelled in the morning, otherwise a quiet day. Patrols & working parties out during the night. No hostile patrols met. Weather fine & warm.	4 men wounded

R.D. Cheales, Lt. Col.
Commdg 17th R Scots.

WAR DIARY

14th ROYAL SCOTS

Army Form C. 2118 — Vol 3

INTELLIGENCE SUMMARY

(Erase heading not required.)

Instructions regarding War Diaries and Intelligence Summaries are contained in F. S. Regs., Part II. and the Staff Manual respectively. Title Pages will be prepared in manuscript.

Place	Date	Hour	Summary of Events and Information	Remarks and references to Appendices
ROUGE du BOUT	April 1st		Battalion in trenches	
			Marched back to Brigade Reserve billets at ROUGE du BOUT, holding two posts CHARRED POST and WINDY POST north of Y Coy trying immediate reserve to Battalion in the trenches. Weather very fine. Warm. (Map sheet 36)	
	4th		Battalion relieved the ROUGE du BOUT by the 20th Fus Yrs. and was relieved at the RUE NEUF BERQUIN. Weather dull but dry. Some warm. Marched by Coys to ESTAIRES area and was relieved at the RUE NEUF BERQUIN. Relief completed by 6.30 pm. The Battalion moved by Coys to ESTAIRES area and was relieved at the RUE NEUF BERQUIN. Weather dull but dry. Some warm.	
	10th		CO and 2nd in Command went into trenches FAUQUISSART section. (Bn H.Q. MOUQMONT HOUSE)	
	11th		O.C. Coys. M.G. Officer & Signalling Officer went up to FAUQUISSART section. The Battalion was inspected by Lieut Gen Sir Charles MONRO, commd'g 1st Army at 4.30pm. Rain most of the day cold & windy	
	12th		Battalion marched up to FAUQUISSART section leaving billets at 6pm and proceeding via LAVENTIE where guides were met at 4.30pm. Relief completed 9.55pm. (Map BETHUNE Combined Sheet). Front trenches (frontage 1700 yards from ROTTEN ROW to FRITH STREET both inclusive) Right Company, W Coy. Reserve platoons Right Centre X Coy reserve one platoon; Left Centre Y Coy; Left Coy Z less 2 sections	3 KILLED 2 DIED OF WOUNDS 6 WOUNDED
			E LGIN POST 1 platoon of W Coy. FAUQUISSART POST 1 platoon X " FELTON POST 2 sections Z "	
			Weather fine. Gentle N.W. breeze. C.O. went to Hospital. Major BILTON took over command.	
	14th 15th		Battalion relieved in trenches by 17th R.W.F. Yrs relief completed 11.45pm. Snow night mild. Bright moon.	
	16th		Battalion marched out of ESTAIRES arriving about 11-45pm. Snow night mild. Bright moon. Proceeded to CROIX BARBEE where we relieved 8th of Kingsown Lancashire Regiments. The 1st platoon leaving at 9.45 am and Bn in 4 Coys. in 4 Coys M 319 Y. Billets at CROIX BARBEE. Relief completed. 2.30 pm 3 men at PENIN MARIAGE. RUE du PUIT and CROIX BARBEE carrying guards of MCO and who are in trenches NEUVE CHAPELLE Section. Weather fine. Y Coy in close support of 18th H.L.I.	

1875 Wt. W593/826 1,000,000 4/15 J.B.C. & A. A.D.S.S./Forms/C. 2118.

Army Form C. 2118

WAR DIARY 14th ROYAL SCOTS.
or
INTELLIGENCE SUMMARY

(Erase heading not required.)

Instructions regarding War Diaries and Intelligence Summaries are contained in F. S. Regs., Part II. and the Staff Manual respectively. Title Pages will be prepared in manuscript.

Place	Date	Hour	Summary of Events and Information	Remarks and references to Appendices
CROIX BARBEE	April 18/19th 1916		C.O. & Coys. M.Officer, Signalling Officer went up to trenches to see their positions. Weather fine. Gassy showers of rain with westerly gale.	
	20th		Battalion relieved 18th H.L.I. on right sub section of left section of NEUVE CHAPELLE section. Guides were met at EUSTON POST and M.32.a.7.7 at 7.30 p.m. Relief completed 9.20 p.m. The frontage held is about 1500 yards. 3 Companies hold front line. 1 Platoon at LANSDOWNE POST. 1 Platoon at PORT ARTHUR. 2 Platoons in reserve at EDGWARE ROAD. 1 section HILLS REDOUBT. Battalion H.Q. foot of HUN STREET on EDGWARE ROAD. Nght fct fine with slight west wind.	1 man killed
	21st		Our artillery opened with salvos at 5 p.m. for about 5 minutes on co-operation with T.Ms, M.Gs and Stokes Guns. Enemy immediately replied with field guns and T.Ms in front line. Some damage done to trenches on the right Companies front. 4 of our men last but 2 T.M. men slightly wounded.	
	22nd		Much rain during night. Enemy artillery opened heavy fire on NEUVE CHAPELLE about 6 & 3 a.m. Rained all day. Quiet.	1 man wounded
	23rd		Quiet day. Enemy's M.Gs very active at night. Weather fine. Gentle west wind.	
	24th		Battalion was relieved in trenches by 18th H.L.I. Relief completed at 10.45 p.m. Battalion returned to billets at CROIX BARBEE. C.O. returned from hospital.	
	28th		Battalion was relieved by 20 Lancashire Fusiliers. Relief completed at 6.45 p.m. and we moved to CROIX MARMUSE. Gas Alarm at 8.15 p.m. Battalion stood to for 2½ hours.	

J. Stewart Collins Major

WAR DIARY
or
INTELLIGENCE SUMMARY

Army Form C. 2118

17th ROYAL SCOTS Vol 4

Place	Date	Hour	Summary of Events and Information	Remarks and references to Appendices
CROIX MARMUSE	1/6 6/5/15	9 0'cl'ks	Battalion was relieved by 13th Cheshires and 4th Croix Marmuse at 5 pm going via Vieille Chapelle & Lacouture to the Ferme du Bois Trenches relieving the 14th Gloucesters. Relief completed 9.55 pm. H.Q. at Sandbag House S.14.b 3.2.	
FERME DU BOIS	7/5		Enemy registered on Rope Trench. An armoured cable laid along front line for telephone communication. Quiet day.	
—	8/5			
—	9/5		Giant Periscope erected nr [behind] Tube Station Post. Light shelling by enemy on our front line parapet.	Casualties 1 Killed 3 wounded
—	10/5		Battalion relieved by 18th H.L.I. and went into billets at Le Touret, nr Vieille Chapelle.	
LE TOURET	14/5			
FERME DU BOIS	15/5 16/5		Relieved 18th H.L.I. in the Ferme du Bois Section. Quiet day.	
—	16/5		Very quiet all day. Wet.	
—	17/5		Heavy shelling with 77 mm on right of our front line and on Rope & French Trench. Very hot. Relieved by 18th H.L.I and returned to billets in Le Touret.	Casualties 10 killed and died of wounds 2 wounded
LESLOBES LE TOURET	19/5		Very misty in mornings and hot later on. Quiet. Leslobes, Le Touret. In billets.	
LESLOBES	22/5/15		Moved to Divisional Reserve. The Archbishop of Canterbury visited the Battalion	

WAR DIARY or **INTELLIGENCE SUMMARY**

Army Form C. 2118

17th ROYAL SCOTS.

BETHUNE Combined Map sheet

Place	Date MAY	Hour	Summary of Events and Information	Remarks and references to Appendices
LES LOBES	22nd to 28th		BILLETS & Divisional Reserve.	
FESTUBERT	28/5		Suddenly ordered to relieve 1/6 Cheshires in "FESTUBERT" Section. Moved from LES LOBES into trenches. Relief completed by 12 midnight. Front line consisting of "islands", not All connected up, nor do Communication trenches join up. All relief for islands to be done by night. 1 Platoon from each Coy. in the front line and GEORGE ST.	
	29/5		Support line lightly shelled by 77 mm & Patrol came into contact with enemy's Trench bombers. dispersed them	Casualties: 1 Officer (2 Lt. Connell) died of wounds. 1 man died of wounds. 2 killed 4 wounded
	30/5		Very heavy artillery bombardment both by our own & Enemy's artillery in the NEUVE CHAPELLE Section. Quiet day otherwise except for a few 77 mm and Rifle grenades on islands.	
	31/5 to 1/6		Quiet day. much work done in wiring in front of islands.	

Army Form C. 2118

WAR DIARY or INTELLIGENCE SUMMARY
(Erase heading not required.)

17th ROYAL SCOTS, Vol 5
Map BETHUNE combined Sheet.

Instructions regarding War Diaries and Intelligence Summaries are contained in F.S. Regs., Part II. and the Staff Manual respectively. Title Pages will be prepared in manuscript.

Place	Date June	Hour	Summary of Events and Information	Remarks and references to Appendices
TRENCHES	1st		Light shelling by enemy of our front parapet. Wiring continued between the islands. Battalion relieved by 18th H.L. Infantry. Relief completed by 11.15 p.m.	
FESTUBERT VILLAGE LINE	2nd		Battalion in support, partly in POSTS, partly in Billets. POSTS, FESTUBERT EAST and Central. LE PLANTIN, and CAILLOUX NORTH and South.	
TRENCHES	5th		Battalion relieved H.L.I. in "A" Relief completed without incident by 10.30 p.m. a Company of 2/6 Gloucester Regt. with C.O. and Adjutant attached to Battalion for instruction.	
"	6th		Quiet day. Large working and wiring parties out at night between the islands.	
"	7th		Front line lightly shelled in evening, otherwise very quiet.	
"	8th		Quiet day. M.G. snipers busy at night. Working & wiring parties did much work.	
"	9th		Attached Troops left.	
"	10th		Wet day, with heavy thunderstorms. No activity on either side.	
"	11th		Battalion relieved by 17th Notts & Derby Regt. Relief complete by 11.30 p.m. Much work done during the tour of the 18th in these trenches in wiring in front of the islands, and improving the communication between them rendering it possible to go from one to the other in most cases by daylight.	
LESBŒUFS	12th		In Divisional Reserve Billets.	
MONT BERNARD CHON	16th		Inspected by Billets at MONT BERNARCHON. The Division being withdrawn from the line into Corps Reserve.	Casualties 2 Killed. 1 wounded.
Near BUSNES	17th		Marched to new Billets about 2 miles off near BUSNES	
OBLINGHEM	18th to 30th		Marched to billets in OBLINGHEM. In billets. Division transferred from Corps Reserve to G.H.Q. Reserve.	

106th Bde.
35th Div.

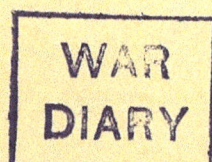

17th BATTALION

THE ROYAL SCOTS

1st to 31st JULY 1916.

Report on Operations 29/30th with G.S. Diary.

WAR DIARY 17th ROYAL SCOTS

35 - July
Army Form C. 2118

INTELLIGENCE SUMMARY
(Erase heading not required.)

Map LENS 11. Vol 6
AMIENS 17

Place	Date July	Hour	Summary of Events and Information	Remarks and references to Appendices
5:6 RS	2nd		Battalion received orders to move. Entrained at CHOCQUES at 11 p.m.	
	3rd		Arrived at FREVENT at 3 a.m. Marched to IVERGNY. Billeted there until July 5th	
	5th	6:30 p.m	Major L.L. BILTON transferred to 9/8th Worcester Regt. 15 company commanding the Bn. Batt marched to BOIS DU WARNIMONT arriving 3:30 a.m. 6th July. Billeted in huts there until 10th July.	
	10th	6 a.m	" to COIGNEUX for attachment to 48th DIV. Orders for this cancelled and Batt. marched	
		3 pm	at 3 pm to VARENNES arriving about 7 pm. Billeted in huts there until 12th July.	
	12th	9 pm	Batt. marched to BRESLE arriving at 1 am. Billets in village	
	13th	10 am	" to BOIS DES CELESTINS arriving about 2:30 p.m. At 6:30 pm marched to BILLON COPSE	
			Bivouacked there.	
	14th	11 am	Batt marched to TALUS BOISE. 106th BDE held in readiness to move forward if required.	
		9 pm	Supplied working party digging trenches at night in the vicinity of WATERLOT FARM.	
	17th	2:30 pm	Lieut-Col R.D. CHEALES comdg. the Batt., Capt R.C. BARRY, and Capt E.E. RUDDELL comdg. Y and X coys respectively wounded by a shell when making a reconnaissance just S. of DELVILLE WOOD. Major G.F. FOULKES assumed	2:30 am wounds Capt BARRY Capt RUDDELL
	19th	5 am	command of the Bat. The Bn moved back to bivouac in CAFTET WOOD	25th killed-2 wounded-3
	20th	9 pm	" night working party digging trench south end of TRONES WOOD	killed-3 wounded-11
	23rd		Another orders from 8th Bde Battn. H.Q. W and X Coys moved forward to BRESLAU TRENCH. Y and Z Coys into MONTAUBAN DEFENCES.	killed-4 wounded-1
	24th		W and X Coys moved forward to N end of BERNAFAY WOOD. Battn H Q. into MONTAUBAN DEFENCES. Later on same date, W and X Coys moved into LONGUEVAL ALLEY and were engaged in clearing the trench.	killed-3 wounded-21
	25th		The Batt. relieved by 20th ROYAL FUSILIERS and returned to bivouac in CAFTET WOOD	wounded-3
	26th		Battalion moved forward into SILESIA front line and support trench	
			Major FOULKES Comdg. the Battalion resigned his command and taken to hospital. Colonel SCOUGAL assumed command of the Battalion.	

1875 Wt. W593/826 1,000,000 4/15 J.B.C. & A. A.D.S.S./Forms/C. 2118.

Army Form C. 2118

MAP AMIENS 17

WAR DIARY
or
INTELLIGENCE SUMMARY
(Erase heading not required.)

Place	Date	Hour	Summary of Events and Information	Remarks and references to Appendices
	27-7-16	5 pm	Batt. returned to bivouac in CAFTET WOOD.	Killed O.R. 5 Wounded 7
	29-7-16		Batt. ordered to take part in attack upon GUILLEMONT - FALFEMONT FARM LINE. moved forward into CASEMENT TRENCH.	
	30-7-16		" " subsequently to BERNAFAY TRENCH and C.T. running from DAWSON TRENCH to MALTZ HORN FARM	Killed 6 Wounded 19 Missing 2
			" " launch an appart upon the 89th Bde. Another advance impossible owing to the number of troops between Batt. and front line. One platoon sent out to reconnoitre MALTZ HORN FARM. Communication with this platoon could not be established but the Battalion was held in readiness to move forward as soon as opportunity occurred.	
		9 pm	Battalion withdrawn returned to bivouac in CAFTET WOOD	

Alex L. Scoular
Captain
Comdg 17th R. Scots

106th Brigade
35th Division.

17th BATTALION

THE ROYAL SCOTS

AUGUST 1 9 1 6

35
Army Form C. 2118
Vol 7

WAR DIARY

17th (Service) Battn. The Royal Scots (Rosebery)

INTELLIGENCE SUMMARY

(Erase heading not required.)

Instructions regarding War Diaries and Intelligence Summaries are contained in F. S. Regs., Part II. and the Staff Manual respectively. Title Pages will be prepared in manuscript.

Place	Date	Hour	Summary of Events and Information	Remarks and references to Appendices
Morlancourt	1-8-16		Battalion moved to MORLANCOURT.	
Suzanne	5-8-16		Battalion moved to SAISSEVAL on train from MERICOURT and SALEUX.	
	10-8-16		Battalion moved back to MORLANCOURT by some route.	
	16-8-16		Battalion moved from MORLANCOURT to SANDPIT VALLEY.	
	20-8-16		Battalion moved from SANDPIT VALLEY to MINDEN POST and bivouaced in CONTOUR WOOD.	
	21-8-16	12 noon	Battalion supplied working party for carrying purposes of 1 Officer and 170 mm to MALTZ HORN TRENCH	
		4 pm		
	22-8-16	8 pm	Battalion moved to trenches. Took over SILESIA TRENCH from 16th Lancs about 10 pm	
	23-8-16		Supplied working party of 10 Officers and 300 mm under Capt A. Douglas	
	24-8-16	11.30am	Party of 4 N.C.O's + 42 men as carriers to 108 M.G. Coy.	1 O.R missing 8" wounded
		12 noon	Party of 4 N.C.O's + 40 men to carry for 106 T.M Battery	
			1 Sergt + 20 men for duty at STRAGGLERS POST.	
		6.30pm	Supplied Working Party of 2 Officers and 60 mm.	Capt Douglas W.A (miss) 2/Lt Fraser H.R (killed)
		1.30am -4 pm	Supplied Working Party of 8 Officers + 300 mm under Capt Douglas	
	25.8.16	9 am	Supplied working party of 2 Officers and 50 mm for carrying purposes Capt + Adjt A.G. Seoval A/comdg Bn	3.2 Runners
			wounded (shell concussion) Taken to Hospital. Capt W Simpson assumed A/comd of Bn	
	26.8.16	11 am	Relieved by 12th Gloucesters and marched to camp at HAPPY VALLEY	
	28-8-16		Major E.T Weston 16th Lancs Fusiliers assumed temporary command of Battn.	
Bernaville	30.8.16		Battalion moved to BERNAVILLE via road and train	
Sus-St-Leger	31.8.16		Battalion moved by road from BERNAVILLE to SUS-ST LEGER	

H. Gellatly Lieut & Adjut
17(S) Batt The Royal Scots

WAR DIARY

INTELLIGENCE SUMMARY

Army Form C. 2118

Vol 8

17th(Service) Battalion Royal Scots (Rockery)

SEPTEMBER.

Place	Date	Hour	Summary of Events and Information	Remarks and references to Appendices
	1st		In billets at SUS. ST LEGER	
	2nd	5.30PM	Batt. moved by motor busses to DUISANS in relief of 15th Durham Light Infantry In billets overnight	
	3rd	7.PM	Batt. moved by road to Arras. In billets overnight.	
	4th	6.A.M	Batt. relieved 18th K.O.Y.L.I. in K.I. Sub-sector ARRAS.	
	10th	9.A.M.	Batt. relieved by 17th WEST YORKSHIRE REGIMENT. Took over billets and posts from 19th DURHAM LIGHT INFANTRY in Brigade Reserve. One Company billeted in ARRAS. One Company in ROCLINCOURT. Dug-outs in ST. NICHOLAS. One and a half Companies in trenches in ROCLINCOURT. One Platoon in THELUS REDOUBT. One platoon in OBSERVATORY POST.	10 OR killed 1 OR wounded
	11th-15th		In billets at ARRAS in Brigade Reserve.	
	16th-22nd	5.30am	Batt. relieved 17.W.YORKS.REGT. in trenches	10 R. killed (Arras) 2 ORs Wounded
	22nd 23rd 27th		Batt. returned by 17th W.YORKS.Regt. and furnished to billets at DUISANS. Batt. in billets at DUISANS and supplies working Parties while in Divisional Reserve.	
	27th	7pm	Batt. moved to billets in ARRAS. and remained three overnight	
	28th 30th	6 am	Batt. relieved 17th W.YORKS.REGT. in trenches	6 ORs wounded

E.J. Hoben Lt Col
Comy 17th Royal Scots

13th (Service) Battn. The Royal Scots (Rosebery)

Army Form C. 2118

Vol 4

WAR DIARY
or
INTELLIGENCE SUMMARY
(Erase heading not required.)

Instructions regarding War Diaries and Intelligence Summaries are contained in F.S. Regs., Part II. and the Staff Manual respectively. Title Pages will be prepared in manuscript.

Place	Date	Hour	Summary of Events and Information	Remarks and references to Appendices
ARRAS.	1-10-16 to 5-10-16		In trenches at ARRAS. Relieved by 17th W. Yorks and moved into BDE RESERVE on 5-10-16.	5 O.Rs. wounded
	6-10-16 to 10-10-16		In BDE RESERVE. Supplies working parties to Posts and FRONT LINE.	
	11-10-16 to 17-10-16		Relieved 17th W. Yorks in trenches. Moved into DIV RESERVE on relief.	1 OR killed 4 " wounded
	18-10-16 to 22-10-16		In DIV RESERVE and supplies working Parties to R.E. on relief.	
	23-10-16 to 29-10-16		Relieved 17th W. Yorks in trenches. On relief moved into BDE RESERVE and SUPPORT LINE. Distribution as follows:- W Coy. in G.H.1.L WORKS. - X Coy. ST NICHOLAS. - Y Coy. ROCLINCOURT. - Z Coy. - EARJ FLWORKS - THELUS POST and OBSERVATORY FORT. - Bn H.Q ARRAS.	6 ORs killed 10 " wounded 5 " wounded at duty.
	30-10-16 to 31-10-16		Supplies working Parties.	

E.U.White Lieut: Col:
Commanding 13th (Service) Batt. The Royal Scots (Rosebery)

WAR DIARY 17th Royal Scots.
or
INTELLIGENCE SUMMARY November 1916.

Army Form C. 2118

Vol 76

Place	Date	Hour	Summary of Events and Information	Remarks and references to Appendices
ARRAS	1/11/16		In Brigade Reserve. Supplying working parties.	E.S.H.C.
ARRAS	2/11/16		In Brigade Reserve. do 3 other ranks wounded	E.S.H.C.
ARRAS	3/11/16		In Brigade Reserve. do	E.S.H.C.
TRENCHES	4/11/16		Quiet day. 2 other ranks died of wounds. 1 other rank wounded.	E.S.H.C.
TRENCHES	5/11/16		Quiet day. 1 other rank wounded. V. wet day	E.S.H.C.
TRENCHES	6/11/16		Enemy heavy T.M. fired 20 rounds, was then silenced by our guns. Wet day.	E.S.H.C.
TRENCHES	7/11/16		Our Rifle grenades did some damage to German working party.	E.S.H.C.
TRENCHES	8/11/16		At 1 A.M. one of enemy shouted to our sentry in No1 Sap. "It's cold to-night Jock". It's cold to-night Jock". 2/Lts W.F. BORTHWICK, M. STEWART and S.C. FALCONER joined for duty	E.S.H.C.
TRENCHES	9/11/16		Enemy sent over a few T.Ms and L.H.V. shells during night. 2/Lt S.F.R. LYELL evacuated sick to UNITED KINGDOM.	E.S.H.C.
ARRAS	10/11/16		To Division Relieved by 17th WEST YORKS. Relief complete 10-50 A.M. Battalion E.S.H.C. marched back to Divisional Reserve in ARRAS	E.S.H.C.

Army Form C. 2118

WAR DIARY
or
INTELLIGENCE SUMMARY

(Erase heading not required.)

Instructions regarding War Diaries and Intelligence Summaries are contained in F. S. Regs., Part II. and the Staff Manual respectively. Title Pages will be prepared in manuscript.

Place	Date	Hour	Summary of Events and Information	Remarks and references to Appendices
ARRAS	11/4/16		In Divisional Reserve. 300 men Works' fouls 15 other ranks joined for duty	25.H.C.
ARRAS	12/4/16		In Divisional Reserve. 300 men Work's fouls	25.H.C.
ARRAS	13/4/16		do	25.H.C.
ARRAS	14/4/16		do	25.H.C.
ARRAS	15/4/16		do CAPTAIN E.A. GODFREY joined for duty.	25.H.C.
TRENCHES	16/4/16		Relieved 1st WEST. YORKS. Relief complete 11 A.M. Enemy put over 65 shots with Heavy T.M. and demolished No 1 Sap to KITE CRATER.	25.H.C.
TRENCHES	17/4/16		Aeroplanes active. A patrol sent to reconnoitre POPE'S NOSE attempted to capture enemy there and one officer got into enemy trench. They were however bombed and obliged to retire. Lieuts W.A. WILLS and S. McKNIGHT wounded, 3 other ranks wounded (other ranks wounded accidentally	

1875 Wt. W593/826 1,000,000 4/15 J.B.C. & A. A.D.S.S./Forms/C. 2118.

Army Form C. 2118

WAR DIARY
or
INTELLIGENCE SUMMARY
(Erase heading not required.)

Instructions regarding War Diaries and Intelligence Summaries are contained in F.S. Regs., Part II. and the Staff Manual respectively. Title Pages will be prepared in manuscript.

Place	Date	Hour	Summary of Events and Information	Remarks and references to Appendices
TRENCHES	18/11/16		Quiet day.	25.M.C.
TRENCHES	19/11/16		Enemy T.M. activity during day.	25.M.C.
TRENCHES	20/11/16		Enemy T.M. activity on Right and Left Company fronts. 2 other ranks wounded.	25.M.C.
TRENCHES	21/11/16		Enemy T.M. activity. 1 other rank killed.	25.M.C.
TRENCHES	22/11/16		Relieved by 17th WEST YORKS. Relief complete 10-45 A.M. To Brigade Reserve. Quiet day. 10 other ranks wounded.	25.M.C.
TRENCHES	23/11/16		In Brigade Reserve. Working parties. MAJOR E.S.K. CROSS joined for duty and assumed command of the Battalion.	25.M.C.
ARRAS	24/11/16		do	25.M.C.
TRENCHES				25.M.C.
ARRAS				
1 ARRAS	25/11/16		do	25.M.C.
ARRAS	26/11/16		do	25.M.C.
ARRAS	27/11/16		do	25.R.R.
ARRAS	28/11/16		Relieved 17th WEST YORKS. Relief complete 11 A.M. 1 other rank wounded.	25.M.C.
TRENCHES	29/11/16		T.M. activity in afternoon.	25.M.C.
TRENCHES	30/11/16		Quiet day.	25.M.C.

E.S.K. Cross Major
Commanding 17th Royal Scots.

Army Form C. 2118

17TH (S) Bn. The ROYAL SCOTS WAR DIARY or INTELLIGENCE SUMMARY

(Erase heading not required.)

Vol XI

Place	Date	Hour	Summary of Events and Information	Remarks and references to Appendices
TRENCHES ARRAS	Dec 1		Bn. in Trenches in K1 Sub Sector, ARRAS. Quiet owing to fog.	Our wire in front strengthened during day
	" 2	10.30AM	Bn. relieved by 11TH R.Scots and returned to billets in ARRAS.	
DAINVILLE		6 PM	Bn. marched to DAINVILLE and billeted there for the night.	
GOUY-EN-TERNOIS	" 3	7 AM	Bn. marched to GOUY-EN-TERNOIS and billeted there.	
	to 7		Remained at GOUY. Co. and Specialist Training carried out daily	
TERNAS	Dec 8	9.30AM	Bn. marched to TERNAS and billeted there	
	" 9	9.30AM	Bn. inspected by Major Genl. H.J.S. LANDON, C.B., comg. 35TH DIV.	
	" 12		Lt. Col. C.B.J. RICCARD assumed command of Bn. vice Major E.G.K.CROSS	
	" 16	11 AM	All men in Bn. considered by O.C.Coy unfit for service in Infantry inspected by G.O.C. VI Corps (Lt. Gen. HALDANE)	(and 125 men marked unfit thereafter by A.D.M.S. 35TH DIV. Specialist and P. Training carried on daily. Each Co. fired a short Musketry Course.
		3.30 PM	Draft of 160 other ranks from 20TH. I.B.D. joined the Bn. These men came from Reserve Cavalry Depot YORK, and were originally ROYAL DRAGOONS and ROYAL SCOTS GREYS.	
	" 20	10.15AM	Bn. inspected by Corps Commander and a large number of additional men rejected as unfit.	
	" 25		Sports held by Bn. in forenoon and afternoon. Xmas Services in the evening, and a concert in the evening	
	" 26	10.15AM	All men (326 in all) rejected as unfit by VI Corps Commander were inspected by G.O.C. Third Army (Gen. Sir Ed. ALLENBY)	
	" 29	2 PM	Bn. moved by motor lorries to ARRAS and relieved 17TH W.YORKS R. New Draft, A.D.M.S. regrets, and 17th W Yorks remained in ARRAS	
ARRAS			32 Signallers (for training) remained in TERNAS. 200 O.R. of 17TH W Yorks remained in ARRAS. Bn. supplied Working parties for N.Z. Tunnelling Co. in caves at ARRAS in three shifts daily as follows:- 6 AM 140 men ; 2 PM 220 men ; 10 PM 140 men	

1875 Wt. W593/826 1,000,000 4/15 J.B.C. & A. A.D.S.S./Forms/C. 2118.

Commanding 17th (Service) Batn. The Royal Scots (Reserve)

WAR DIARY or INTELLIGENCE SUMMARY

17TH (S) BN. The Royal Scots

Army Form C. 2118

Place	Date	Hour	Summary of Events and Information	Remarks and references to Appendices
ARRAS	1917 1st Jan. 2nd 4th 6th 13th 17th 18th 20th 24th 26th 31st		Bn. in billets. Daily Working Parties for N.Z. Tunnelling Co. R.E. 500 men employed. 115 A.D.M.S. inspection sent to Baths. Draft which joined Bn. on 18.12.16 sent to Depot Bn. 35TH DIV. Raid by 9th DIV on enemy trenches opposite ARRAS. Heavy bombardment by our Artillery. No reply on ARRAS. Capt R. DEDGAR with 4 Sub. Officers and 4 N.C.O Instructors TO TERNAS to train new drafts arriving there. 54. O.R. reinforcements arrived. 119. O.R. and 83 O.R. reinforcements arrived. 28 O.R. reinforcements arrived. 123 O.R. " " 50 O.R. " " 283 O.R. rejects as unfit by G.O.C. Third Army sent to Base, at HAVRE, ETAPLES, ROUEN, and 3rd Can. Div. Tunnelling Co. Additional Officer and N.C.O. Instructors sent from ARRAS to TERNAS Major C.F.F. FOULKES to TERNAS to take command of detachment. Notification received of following Honours and Awards notes in the London Gazette. "Mentioned in Despatches" Lt.Col R.D.CHEALES 22622 Corpl. A.STEPHEN "Awarded Military Cross" 24905 Pte J. BOWERS " " Meritorious Service Medal" 21944 Co. St. Major P. KERR 24774 Corpl. J. Mc MORRAN. No 24781 Pte B McCLONE wounded slightly by shrapnel when in billets. The only casualty in the Bn during their spell in ARRAS.	Following Officers joined during month 2/LIEUT. COATS, W.E. 4.1.17 " BLACKIE, J. 9.1.17 " THOMSON, J. 9.1.17 " MERRILEES, A.J. 10.1.17 " STRUTH, J.S. 10.1.17 " JOHNSTONE, R.H. 10.1.17 " THURSTONE, A 10.1.17 Capt. RUDDELL, 14.1.17 2/Lt MILLER, W. 16.1.17 " WADDELL, J.H. 16.1.17 " STEWART, J.B. " " THORNTON, J.T. " Capt. MITCHELL, J.H. 24.1.17 2/Lt. NOBLE, W.B. 24.1.17

C.M. Accredible
Col 17th Royal Scots

Army Form C. 2118

Unit: 17TH (S) BN THE ROYAL SCOTS.   **WAR DIARY** or **INTELLIGENCE SUMMARY**

(Erase heading not required.)

Instructions regarding War Diaries and Intelligence Summaries are contained in F.S. Regs., Part II. and the Staff Manual respectively. Title Pages will be prepared in manuscript.

Place	Date	Hour	Summary of Events and Information	Remarks and references to Appendices
ARRAS	1-2-17	-	Bn. in Billets in ARRAS. Supplied working parties to N.Z. Tunnelling Co.	2/Lt A. NIVEN A. posted to Bn. on 26.2.17
"	2-2-17	-	Bn. moved by March Route to billets at WANQUETIN. Billeted there for night.	
"	3-2-17	-	Bn. moved by March Route to billets at GOUY-EN-TERNOIS.	
GOUY-EN-TERNOIS	6-2-17	-	Bn. " " " " GRAND-BEURET. Billeted there overnight.	
"	7-2-17	-	Bn. " " " " GERAINCOURT.	
VIGNACOURT	8-2-17	-	Bn. " " " " VIGNACOURT.	
"	19-2-17	1 PM	Accidental Bomb explosion during training. (2 O.R. Killed, 6 O.R. wounded).	
"	19/2-2-17		Bn/Somerport moved by road en route for MARCELCAVE	
"			Bn. moved by train to MARCELCAVE. In Billets.	
MARCELCAVE	22-2-17		Bn. moved by road to CAMP DECAUVILLE, near BEAUCOURT.	
"			10. O.R. reinforcements arrived from 20.I.B.D.	
"	24-2-17		1 Off + 101 O.R. proceeding to ann Railhead Beaucourt as Permanent Working Party.	
"	25-2-17		1 Off + 30 O.R. reinforcements arrived from 20th I.B.D.	
"	26-2-17		Bn. moved to Bde RESERVE in LIHONS Sector In Billets in ROSIERES.	
"			7. O.R's of Draft which arrived on 22nd inst, having been rejected by ADMS. 35th Div. on 23rd inst proceeded to join 20.I.B.D.	
"			1 Off + 104 O.R. proceeded to Musketry Camp, PONT REMY.	

Army Form C. 2118

17th (S) Bn The ROYAL SCOTS   WAR DIARY
INTELLIGENCE SUMMARY
(Erase heading not required.)

Instructions regarding War Diaries and Intelligence Summaries are contained in F.S. Regs., Part II. and the Staff Manual respectively. Title Pages will be prepared in manuscript.

Place	Date	Hour	Summary of Events and Information	Remarks and references to Appendices
ROSIERES	March 1917 1st		Bn. in billets in Bde Reserve in ROSIERES.	
TRENCHES	2nd 3rd to 6th		Bn. relieved 18th HIGH L.I. in left sub sector of the LIHONS Sector. Relief completed at 10.30 p.m. Bn. HQ in BOIS TRIANGULAIRE. Trenches in very bad condition, mud being waist deep in places. Most of the time was spent in endeavouring to clear the C.Ts., also the front line by working laterally from sentry groups. A heavy snow storm on night of 4th/5th greatly hindered the work. Enemy Artillery and T.Ms were active on our Rt Co. front in vicinity of LIHONS-CHAULNES Road, things otherwise quiet on the whole.	Casualties Killed: 4 O.R. Wounded: 9 O.R.
	6th/7th		Bn relieved by 18th HIGH L.I. Relief completed by 12:15 AM on 7th. Bn. relieved 17th W. YORKS R. in Bde. Support. Relief completed by 10.5 p.m.	
	7th to 9th		Bn. HQ at junction of IRIS and SELENITES Trenches. Advanced BnHQ in CAROLINE TR. in BOIS MIEG. Cos. in IRIS TR. less 2 Platoons X Co in BOIS MIEG and 2 L.Gs. attached to 17th W YORKS R. in LA DEMI LUNE. A quiet tour for Bn except for enemy T.Ms firing on 17th when enemy under cover of an intense bombardment raided 17th W YORKS R in LA DEMI LUNE. about 7 p.m. 1 L.G. belonging to 17 R SCOTS + WYORKS R was lost, supposed to be destroyed by enemy bombardment. During this bombardment Bn stood to and prepared to reinforce front line if required. After the raid 2 Platoons Y Co reinforced X Co 17 W YORKS R. and remained in front line for remainder of tour.	Casualties WOUNDED 3 O.R. MISSING 1 O.R. (A Lewis Gunner in DEMI LUNE and presumed since night of enemy raid)
ROSIERES	9th		Bn relieved by 16th HIGH L.I. (by 10.5 PM) and marched to billets in ROSIERES Bn relieved 23rd Bn MANCHESTER REGT of (late portion of) 17 W YORKS R owing to readjustment in Right Sub Sector, LIHONS Sector. Relief greatly delayed by very bad condition of trenches, and made from this cause to be completed until following evening.	Casualties Killed 1 O.R. WOUNDED 11 O.R.
TRENCHES	10th 10th to 14th		Bn. HQ in P.C. HENNEQUIN. Most of the trenches practically impassable owing to active but on the alert, our patrols being frequently fired on. Enemy T.Ms active against BOIS FREDERIC in Centre Co. (Z) Front but did little damage. A good deal of rain at nights made the	

Army Form C. 2118

WAR DIARY
17th (S) Bn The ROYAL SCOTS
INTELLIGENCE SUMMARY
(Erase heading not required.)

Instructions regarding War Diaries and Intelligence Summaries are contained in F.S. Regs., Part II. and the Staff Manual respectively. Title Pages will be prepared in manuscript.

Place	Date	Hour	Summary of Events and Information	Remarks and references to Appendices
TRENCHES ROSIERES	MARCH 1917 14/15		Bn. relieved by 15th Bn. CHESHIRE REGT. Relief completed at 5.15 AM on 15th. Bn. marched to billets in ROSIERES and at 4 PM same day marched to huts at CAMP DES BALLONS.	
CAMP DES BALLONS	16th & 17th		Cleaning up, bathing and after the trenches, and training. Reinforcements of 41 O.R. arrived from Base.	
	17th		News received of German withdrawal from front line in IV Corps front. Bn. marched at 10 PM. to billets in ROSIERES.	
ROSIERES				
TRENCHES	18th		Bn. marched at 9 AM to positions in the British and German front lines in Right Subsector of LIHONS Sector. 2 Platoons W/pers Z Coy in the German line, remainder and X Coy in the British line. Bn. HQ at P.C. HENNEQUIN	
HALLU ROUVROY	19th		Bn. moved at 5 AM to HALLU and took up position in trenches. At 5.30 PM Bn. marched to ROUVROY for Salvage work. Bn. quartered for night in cellars, ruins &c.	
ROSIERES	20th		Bn. moved at 8 AM to ROSIERES. Salvage work having been cancelled, for work on ROSIERES-CHAULNES Railway	
	20th to 28th		In billets in ROSIERES. Daily working parties of whole Bn, for first 2 days engaged in repairing Railway and later in repairing LIHONS-CHAULNE-OMIECOURT Road.	
	22nd 23rd		Reinforcement of 20 O.R. from Base. LT. COL. R.D. CHEALES rejoined the Bn. and resumed command.	
LICOURT	29th		Bn. marched to LICOURT and billets in ruins there. Working Parties repairing roads and filling in mine craters.	
Y and CROIX-MOLIGNAUX	30th		Bn. marched to Y and CROIX-MOLIGNAUX and billets in ruins of those villages, Bn. HQ, Y and Z Coys in CROIX-MOLIGNAUX and W & X Coy in Y. All villages have been burnt or destroyed by the retiring enemy, and our troops are quartered in cellars and shelters in the ruins. While Bn. on daily working parties repairing roads.	

R.D. Cheales Lt Col
Comdg 17th (S) Bn The Royal Scots

Army Form C. 2118

17th (S) Bn. The ROYAL SCOTS WAR DIARY
INTELLIGENCE SUMMARY

APRIL 1917

Instructions regarding War Diaries and Intelligence Summaries are contained in F.S. Regs., Part II. and the Staff Manual respectively. Title Pages will be prepared in manuscript.

(Erase heading not required.)

Place	Date	Hour	Summary of Events and Information	Remarks and references to Appendices
CROIX-MOLIGNAUX	APRIL 1917 1st to 8th		In billets. Working parties repairing roads between Y and MONCHY LAGACHE supplied daily. Whole Bn. being employed on this work.	
MONCHY LAGACHE	9th	2 pm	Bn. marched to MONCHY LAGACHE and billeted there for the night 9th/10th.	
SOYÉCOURT	10th	9 am	Bn. marched to SOYÉCOURT into Bde. Support. Bn. remained in SOYÉCOURT till 12th Apr.	
FRONT LINE near SOYÉCOURT	12th to 16th	2.30 pm	Bn. took over part of 104th Bde front line between LES VERGUIERS and River OMIGNON, South of River OMIGNON, immediately South of River OMIGNON, Right Bn. of 106th Bde. Approx. line held by Bn. is shown on attached map. Outposts Advanced posts were pushed out as opportunity offered and shown on attached map by Red Circles with date of their establishment. Patrolling was carried out nightly, through BERTHAUCOURT (reported by our patrols on 13.4.17 as evacuated by the enemy) in the direction of PONTRUET and to South of these villages. R. HQ in MAISSEMY. Bn. relieved by 16th HIGH. L.I. and moved into Bde Reserve at VERMAND.	CASUALTIES KILLED:- 6 O.R. WOUNDED:- Capt E.E. RUDGE 2/Lt J.C. FALCONER 18 O.R.
VERMAND	16th to 19th		In billets in VERMAND. Working Parties supplied daily for repair roads in vicinity.	
FRONT LINE near BERTHAUCOURT	20th to 23rd		Bn. relieved 18th HIGH. L.I. in /BERTHAUCOURT Sector, holding same line as before, viz 2 Coys on line marked A-B on attached map. 1 Co. in support in valley marked C, and 1 Co. in reserve in MAISSEMY. Operations same as previous tour, viz improvement of line A-B, patrolling and pushing out advanced posts as opportunity offered.	KILLED:- 1 O.R. WOUNDED:- 8 O.R.
	23rd		Bn. relieved by 17th LANC. FUS. and marched to VILLEVEQUE into Div. Reserve.	

1875 Wt. W593/826 1,000,000 4/15 J.B.C. & A. A.D.S.S./Forms/C. 2118.

Army Form C. 2118

17(S) Bn The Royal Scots WAR DIARY
(Continued) INTELLIGENCE SUMMARY   APRIL 1917

(Erase heading not required.)

Instructions regarding War Diaries and Intelligence Summaries are contained in F.S. Regs., Part II. and the Staff Manual respectively. Title Pages will be prepared in manuscript.

Place	Date	Hour	Summary of Events and Information	Remarks and references to Appendices
VILLEVEQUE	APRIL 1917 23rd 5-29th		Bn in DIV Reserve. Working Parties on roads and Bn. Training carried on on alternate days.	
MAISSEMY	30th	2 pm	Bn marched to MAISSEMY in Bde Reserve to 18th HIGH L.I. who were holding front line from Hill 120 (M14 d ref. Maf. 1/20000 Sheet 62B S.W.) to FRESNOY LE PETIT - GRICOURT Road. Bn HQ + 1 Co. in MAISSEMY : 3 Cos in valley just between MAISSEMY and VILLECHOLLES.	

Strength of Bn on 1st April 1917 was 47 Officers and 853 Other Ranks
 "   "   "   " 30th   "   "   " 36   "   " 869   "   "
Reinforcements during April were received as follows :- 7.4.17. 62 Other Ranks
                                                        25.4.17. 14   "   "

On 13.4.17 Lt Col. R.D. CHEALES relinquished command of the Bn owing to ill health, and was succeeded in command of the Bn by Major S. HUFFAM, 19th (S) Bn. DURH. L.I.

J. Huffam. Major
Comdg 17(S) Bn The Royal Scots

BELLENGLSE

ST. QUENTIN CANAL

PONTRUET.

BERTHAUCOURT.

R. OMIGNON

PONTRU.

To MAISSEMY 1 Km.

Map 1/20,000
Sheet 62 B S.W.

WAR DIARY or INTELLIGENCE SUMMARY

Army Form C. 2118.

17(3) Bn The ROYAL SCOTS.

MAY, 1917.

17 R Scots 96/16

Place	Date	Hour	Summary of Events and Information	Remarks and references to Appendices
MAISSEMY	May 1st-3rd		Bn in brigade support to 18th H.L.I. in the left sub-sector of the FRESNOY-LE-PETIT sector (vid. WAR DIARY for APRIL, 1917)	1/5/17 2/Lt J.R. HADDOW. gsw.arm. Casualties: 3
FRONT LINE N.W. of FRESNOY	May 3rd-8th		Bn. relieved 18th H.L.I. in above sub-sector; inter-battalion relief completed without incident at 11 p.m. Active patrolling carried out nightly; improvement of front line on. On early morning of 6th three patrols demonstrated against copses in M17 (ref. map 1/20,000 sheet 62 b S.W.) to create a diversion from attack by 19th D.L.I. on strong points in and round LES TROIS SAUVAGES (east of GRICOURT).	killed (att. T.M.B) 6/5/17 Casualties – 2 killed, 6 wounded, 1 wounded at duty.
VILLÉVÈQUE	May 8th-12th		Bn relieved by 16th CHESHIRES and marched into Div. reserve billets in VILLÉVÈQUE. Training carried out and parties engaged on work on roads etc. in vicinity.	9/5/17 Maj. HUFFAM relinquished command of Bn. 10/5/17 Maj. P.S. HALL D.S.O., 15th CHES R. assumed command.
VILLE-CHOLLES	May 14th-18th		Bn moved into billets in VILLECHOLLES in support to 105th Bde and supplies working parties on roads etc.	12/5/17 2/Lt G.J.F. ROBISON rejoined.
TERTRY	May 18th		Bn moved into billets in TERTRY and remained there overnight 18th/19th.	13/5/17 Maj. R.E.M. HEATHCOTE joined.
PERONNE	May 19th-20th		Bn moved into billets in FLAMICOURT a small suburb of PERONNE.	
TEMPLEUX-LA-FOSSE	May 21st-23rd		"Y" coy moved to TEMPLEUX-LA-FOSSE and arranged camp there for Bn. Bn moved to camp near TEMPLEUX-LA-FOSSE and carried out training etc.	

Army Form C. 2118

17th (S) Bn The ROYAL SCOTS (continued)

WAR DIARY
INTELLIGENCE SUMMARY
(Erase heading not required.)

MAY 1917

Place	Date	Hour	Summary of Events and Information	Remarks and references to Appendices
	May 23rd -26th		Bn moved into Bde Reserve in the VILLERS-GUISLAIN sector relieving 21st MIDDLESEX R. Dispositions: 1½ coys in HEUDICOURT, Bn. H.Q. and 3½ coys along railway entrenchment in X 13 and 19a (ref map 1/10,000, sheet 57c S.E. 4). Working parties on roads etc supplied to R.E.	20/5/17 2/Lt J.R. CRAIG joined Bn. 22/5/17 2/Lt W.R. DU 21365 Sgt. J CHALMEY 21614 Sgt. J HARVEY (attd) TMB
VILLERS-GUISLAIN (front line sector)	May 26th		Bn moved into the line relieving 18th H.L.I. in the right sub-sector of the VILLERS-GUISLAIN sector. Dispositions:- Bn. H.Q. in VILLERS-GUISLAIN, one coy in reserve at Xroads in sunken road in X 9 d and X 15 b, one coy in support in sunken road in X 16 a and trench in X 16 d and 2 coys in line from X 17 central to X 11 a 77. Active patrolling with approx objectives HONNECOURT WOOD and roads leading to LES TRANCHEES carried out. Improvement of line and defences carried on.	"Mentioned Dispatches" Sir D. HAIG C-in-C. 31/5/17 Casualties 1 O.R. killed 1 wounded

Bn. strength. 1/5/17 – 38 offrs. 884 O.Rs.
" " 31/5/17 – 41 " 860 "

DRAFTS. 28/5/17 10 O.R. from 20th I.B.D.
20/5/17   6 "   "   "   "   "
3/5/17   9 "   "   "   "   "
         ___
         25

N.W. Hogg Lt Col.
Commanding, 17th Royal Scots.

17th (S) Bn. The Royal Scots   WAR DIARY   JUNE 1917   Army Form C. 2118.

Instructions regarding War Diaries and Intelligence Summaries are contained in F.S. Regs., Part II. and the Staff Manual respectively. Title pages will be prepared in manuscript.

INTELLIGENCE SUMMARY.
(Erase heading not required.)

Vol 17

Place	Date	Hour	Summary of Events and Information	Remarks and references to Appendices
FRONT LINE near VILLERS-GUISLANS	JUNE 1st & 2nd		Relieved in Front Line trenches on 2nd by 15TH CHESHIRES. Bn marched on relief to AIZICOURT-LE-BAS and encamped there.	HONOURS & AWARDS MILITARY CROSS Capt. A.G. SCOUGAL 6/6/17
AIZICOURT-LE-BAS	3rd to 9th		Bn in Camp. Usual training carried on daily. Lt.Col. R.E.M. HEATHCOTE (ROYAL SCOTS) assumed command of Bn on 7th vice Lt.Col. P.S. HALL posted to command 17TH WEST YORKS.	
HEUDICOURT	10th to 17th		Bn moved to Bde Support in GAUCHE WOOD Sector. Bn HQ was encamped near HEUDICOURT 2 Coys. in BROWN LINE (W.11.d.) one in MORRIS BANK (X7a) one in IRVINE LANE (W.12b) Working parties supplied nightly for work on front line trenches	Casualties 13.6.17 WOUNDED: 4 O.R.
FRONT LINE trenches near GONNELIEU	18th to 26th		Relieved 18TH H.L.I. in front line. Bn HQ LINE, 2 Coys in support near KITCHEN CRATER (R.33.28.6) 2 Coys other VILLERS GUISLANS (X 26 7 3) in FRONT A very quiet spell in the trenches. On nights of 23rd/24th and 25th/26th a new trench (marked on attached map A---B) was dug in front of existing front line by 18th H.L.I. and 19th D.L.I. Bn. supplied covering parties and wiring parties. All the front of the new trench was wired during these 2 nights with a double belt of wire. Rayons secaneaux T.M. and Artillery Activity very great during this tour. Patrolling was carried on constantly by us, also deepening and improving Bn. relieved by 14th GLOUCESTERS and marched to Camp in AIZICOURT-LE-BAS	15.6.17 KILLED: 3 O.R. 19/6/17 WOUNDED: 4 O.R. 20.6.17 WOUNDED: 2 O.R. 25.6.17 KILLED: 1 O.R. WOUNDED: 2 O.R. 26.6.17 KILLED: 1 O.R.
AIZICOURT LE BAS	27th to 30th		Bn in Camp. Usual training carried on daily.	

Strength of Bn on 1.6.17 - 41 Officers and 860 Other Ranks
    "   "   "   "   30.6.17 - 41 "   "   623 "   "
Reinforcements: 13.6.17 - 6 O.R.S   25.6.17 2nd Lt D.M. WEATHERSTONE ⎱ Joined Bn.
                    21.6.17 - 10 O.R.   A.T. TAIT   ⎰
                                                                 W. JOHNSTONE

REF. MAP 1/20000 SHEET 57'SE

SQUARE R.34

REFERENCE
ROADS = = = =
BANKS ....
TRENCH ————
WIRE ++++++

(A-B NEW TRENCH
(" " WIRE)

TO BANTEUX → 2 km

TURNER QUARRY

CROOK QUARRY

A

NEWTON POST.

B

TO VILLERS GUISLAIN

TO GONNELIEU

N ←

.5 km

1.5 km

17th (S) Bn. The Royal Scots WAR DIARY JULY 1917

Army Form C. 2118.

Instructions regarding War Diaries and Intelligence Summaries are contained in F.S. Regs., Part II. and the Staff Manual respectively. Title pages will be prepared in manuscript.

INTELLIGENCE SUMMARY.
(Erase heading not required.)

Vol 13

Place	Date JULY	Hour	Summary of Events and Information	Remarks and references to Appendices
TEMPLEUX-LA-FOSSE	1st		In Camp. Bn. Training.	**Casualties**
LONGAVESNES	2nd		Bn. marched to Camp near LONGAVESNES. In camp there until 5th. Daily Training	13.7.17. Wounded: 2 ORs
LEMPIRE	6th to 14th		Bn. in Bde Support in C2 Sub sector. Whole Bn. on night working parties – wiring Bde front and digging new trench between GILLEMONT FARM and CAT POST.	15.7.17. K:- 1 OR. W:- 2
FRONT LINE	14th		Relieved 18th HIGH. L.I. in front line. Dispositions: front line. 1 Co. in GILLEMONT FARM	20.7.17. K:- 1 OR. W:- 4 ORs
TRENCHES			One Co. in D. E. & F. Posts. Support. Rt Sup. Co. in KEN ROAD. Left Sup. Co. in SART LANE. Bn HQ in LEMPIRE. Patrolling nightly on whole Bn front. Enemy seldom in front of our wire, but artillery and T.M. active especially on GILLEMONT FARM.	22.7.17 K:- 1 OR W:- 2 ORs
C2 Sub Sector	19th		Attempted enemy raid on GILLEMONT FARM (along with attempted enemy raid on Bn on our right) after heavy bombardment of the FARM. Raiding parties easily repulsed by Rifle and L.G. Fire and bombs without either reaching our trenches.	**HONOURS** Wounded in 35th DIV Special Orders.
	22nd		Bombarded enemy front line at GILLEMONT FARM from 2.50 am to 3.15 am with Rifle Grenades with good results. Enemy quiet thereafter.	Lt. S. McKNIGHT 2/Lt H. HOUSTON 2/Lt A.T. TAIT
	23rd		Bn. relieved by 15th CHESHIRES and marched to Camp at TEMPLEUX-LA-FOSSE.	22041 Sgt J. SPROULE 24707 Cpl. C. KERR 25068 L/Cpl J. KENNEDY
TEMPLEUX-LA-FOSSE	24th to 31st		In camp at TEMPLEUX-LA-FOSSE. Daily Bn Training.	20. O. Rs.
			Bn Strength on 1/7/17 :- 41 officers 823 O.Rs. " 31/7/17 :- 42 " 799 "	Officers passed { Major G.F.F. FOULKES during month { 2nd Lt D.G. EDNIE

Alex George Major
M/Bn 17 R. Scots

Army Form. C. 2118.

17th (S) Bn. The Royal Scots.

WAR DIARY

INTELLIGENCE SUMMARY
(Erase heading not required.)

AUGUST
Page 1.

Instructions regarding War Diaries and Intelligence Summaries are contained in F. S. Regs., Part II. and the Staff Manual respectively. Title pages will be prepared in manuscript.

Place	Date	Hour	Summary of Events and Information	Remarks and references to Appendices
LEMPIRE	1/8/17		Battn. marched from AIZECOURT-LE-BAS and relieved the 15th Cheshire Regt. in the 15th Sherwood 4forester in C2 Subsector (GILLEMONT FM)	M.C. 2/Lt F.A. RAYNER D.C.M. 40650 Cpl McPHERSON M.M. 40516 Sgt M°PHAIL 248216 Pte WILLIAMS 4088 Pte PRIOR
	6/8/17	4.30 am	Enemy raided GILLEMONT FM defences, caused several casualties and was repulsed with loss. (Honours & awards received in Bn margin)	Casualties 3/8/17 1 or. wounded 5/8/17 1 or. wounded 6/8/17 4 OR wounded 1 " " (accidentally) 2/Lt Grahame wounded on duty 2 or. missing 1 or. killed 10/8/17 4 or. wounded 13/4/17 1 or. wounded (accidentally)
	14/8/17 to 16/8/17		Battn. was relieved by 17th W. Yorks and moved into Bde support in LEMPIRE. Special wiring parties of 2 offs and 100 OR. moved to LONGAVESNES for training in their work. Working parties to front line supplies.	
	17/8/17		Battn. was relieved by 17th W. Yorks in support (less one company) and moved to Bde Reserve in camp near VILLERS-FAUCON. 1 coy moved into the front line in BIRDCAGE subsector.	
	18/8/17 to 24/8/17		In camp. Supplied working and wiring parties to assist 18th HLI in consolidating their gains after attack of 19/8/17 in enemy trenches east of GILLEMONT FM. 1 coy moved into support of GILLEMONT Subsector and 1 coy rejoined Battn from BIRDCAGE. (21/8/17) 1 coy from support in GILLEMONT Subsector rejoined Battn 23/8/17	
	25/8/17		Battn. moved into close support of GILLEMONT subsector in LEMPIRE on account of unsuccessful enemy counter-attack in that sub. sector.	
	24/8/17		Battn. relieved 19th D.L.I. in GILLEMONT subsector	
	30/8/17		Battn. less 2 coys was relieved by 19th D.L.I. 1 coy remained in front line (CAT post) and 1 in support in KEN LANE.	

17th (S) Bn. The Royal Scots.

WAR DIARY
or
INTELLIGENCE SUMMARY.

Army Form C. 2118.

Page 2

Place	Date	Hour	Summary of Events and Information	Remarks and references to Appendices
LEMPIRE	31/8/17		The coy in CAT post and that in KEN LANE were relieved during the morning and in the evening the Battn relieved the 17th W/Yorks on the KNOLL subsector.	14/8/17 1 or. died of wounds 4 or wounded at duty 10 or wounded 1 or killed 20/8/17 8 or wounded 3 or " (at duty) 1 or died of wounds 22/8/17 3 or wounded 1 or " (at duty) 23/8/17 2 or killed 1 or died of wounds 5 or wounded 10 " 24/8/17 2 or killed 1 or wounded at duty 25/8/17 5 or wounded 1 or " at duty 27/8/17 1 or wounded 1 or " (at duty) 28/8/17 2 or wounded

Strength of Battn 1/8/17 :- 42 officers 796 other ranks
              "   31/8/17 :- 42   "   811   "   "

Drafts received   99 other ranks 20/8/17
                  10   "   "   27/8/17
                   6   "   "   28/8/17

29/8/17
1 or wounded
30/8/17
1 or wounded
31/8/17
3 or wounded

M.S.M. Heathcote Lt. Col.
Comdg 17th R. Scots.

Army Form C. 2118.

WAR DIARY
of
17th (S) Bn The Royal Scots

INTELLIGENCE SUMMARY.
(Erase heading not required.)

September 1917

Instructions regarding War Diaries and Intelligence Summaries are contained in F.S. Regs. Part II. and the Staff Manual respectively. Title pages will be prepared in manuscript.

Place	Date	Hour	Summary of Events and Information	Remarks and references to Appendices
LEMPIRE	1/9/17		Battn was relieved by 15th Sherwood Foresters in KNOLL subsector and moved to camp near TEMPLEUX-LA-FOSSE	1.9.17 1 O.R. wounded
TEMPLEUX-LA-FOSSE	2/9/17 to 6/9/17		In camp in Divl. Reserve. Training carried on as usual.	5.9.17 2 O.R. wounded 10.9.17 1 O.R. wounded 14.9.17
EPEHY	6/9/17		Battn relieved 2 coys of 23rd Manchester R. and 2 coys of 18th Lanc. Fusiliers in OSSUS subsector.	4 O.R. wounded 1 O.T. killed 15.9.17
	16/9/17		Raid on enemy trench S. of CANAL WOOD. At least 8 of the enemy men killed and 1 wounded prisoner of 16th B.J.R. captured.	4 O.T. wounded 2/Lt J.S. STRUTH killed 27.9.17
TEMPLEUX-LA-FOSSE	18/9/17		Battn was relieved by 16th Cheshire R. and moved to camp near TEMPLEUX-LA-FOSSE. In camp in Divl. Reserve. Training carried on as usual.	1 O.T. killed 16.9.17 2/Lt F.F. SMITH posted from 1/1 or L.W.B. Horse.
ST. EMILIE	18/9/17 to 26/9/17		Moved into Bde Reserve in GILLEMONT subsector. Working parties to front line and on roads etc supplied. 1 officer and 229 o.r. were attached to R.E. and Tramelling Coy for work on dugouts etc in front line.	
	26/9/17 to 30/9/17			

17th (S) Bn. The Royal Scots   WAR DIARY   Army Form C. 2118.

INTELLIGENCE SUMMARY   September 1917   Page 2

Place	Date	Hour	Summary of Events and Information	Remarks and references to Appendices
			Reinforcements	Honours and rewards.
			1/9/17 — 98 other ranks	40547 S/Sgt (a/sgt) W. HAYNES
			8/9/17 — " 6 " "	40522 L/Sgt W. B. DONALDSON
			16/9/17 — " 97 " "	400887 L/Sgt T. LEY
			25/9/17 — " 52 " "	40943 A/L.Cpl T. NEALLY awarded M.M.
			Strength 1/9/17 — 42 officers 811 other ranks	
			" 30/9/17 — 40 " 1057 " "	

W.J.J. Hannant(?) Mantle(?) Lt.Col.
Comdg 17th R. Scots

Army Form C. 2118.

WAR DIARY
INTELLIGENCE SUMMARY

(Erase heading not required.)

17 R/of (?) October 1917

Instructions regarding War Diaries and Intelligence Summaries are contained in F.S. Regs., Part II. and the Staff Manual respectively. Title pages will be prepared in manuscript.

Place	Date	Hour	Summary of Events and Information	Remarks and references to Appendices
ST EMILIE	1-10-17	—	In Bde Reserve in GUILLEMONT FM - CAT POST Sector	Casualties
TEMPLEUX LA	2-10-17	3 p.m.	Bn moved to Camp at TEMPLEUX LA FOSSE on relief by 9th Bn Kings Liverpool & arrived there morning 3/10.	2/Lt D.G. EDNIE Wounded - 19-10-17
FOSSE	3-10-17	2 p.m.	Bn moved by Motor Lorries to PERONNE and billeted there former night.	Lt. W.D. SIM Wounded 18-10-17 2/Lt C.T. THORNTON Wounded 18-10-17
PERONNE	4-10-17	11.45 p.m.	Bn moved by Train to ARRAS. On arrival at ARRAS at 5.30 am on 5-10-17 Bn marched to camp at DUISANS.	Capt F.M. MITCHELL Died of Wounds 26-10-17 Lt. W. HOUSTON Killed - 24-10-17
DUISANS	5-10-17 to 12-10-17		Bn in Camp at DUISANS training & conducting Specialist training areas carried out.	3/Lt W.E. CATS Wounded - 24-10-17
do	13-10-17	9 p.m.	Bn moved to ARRAS and entrained there for CASSEL. Bn marched to billets at HOGENHILL.	15-10-17 - 3 Ors Wounded 18-10-17 - 2 " Killed 20-10-17 - 65 " Wounded 21-10-17 - 2 " do 22-10-17 - 5 " do 23-10-17 - 2 " do 24-10-17 - 6 " Wounded 25-10-17 - 16 " Wounded 3 " Killed 26-10-17 - 1 " do 28-10-17 - 1 " do 29-10-17 - 1 (killed died) os. 30-10-17 - 1 wounded
HOGENHILL	14-10-17 to 15-10-17		Bn in Billets at HOGENHILL. Training carried out on manual.	
do	16-10-17	7.20 a.m.	Bn moved to ARNEKE Station and entrained for PROVEN. On arrival marched to Camp at R.4, PROVEN AREA and encamped there for the night.	Honours Lt. (A/Major) A.D. LOST MILITARY X. CROSS
PROVEN	19-10-17	6.30 p.m.	Bn moved by road to DEWIPDE CAMP & came into Divnl Reserve.	40547 Sgt W. HAYNES 40322 L/Cpl W.M. DONALDSON 40517 " T. LEY 41943 Cpl T. NEALLY MILITARY MEDALS
TRENCHES	19-10-17	4 p.m.	Bn relieved 23rd Manchesters in the XIV Corps Divnl Reserve at FORET D'HOUTHUST.	
"	20-10-17		Bn were relieved by 23rd Manchesters and moved into Bde Reserve in WOOD 16.	
"	21-10-17	9 p.m.	Bn relieved 17th L. Fusiliers in the Line as on 15th inst.	

T2134. Wt. W708—776. 500000. 4/15. Sir J.C. & S.

WAR DIARY
or
INTELLIGENCE SUMMARY.
(Erase heading not required.)

Army Form C. 2118.

Place	Date	Hour	Summary of Events and Information	Remarks and references to Appendices
TRENCHES	24-10-17	9 p.m.	Bn relieved in line by 1st 4 L.I.	
	26-10-17	4 a.m.	Bn moved by train from EVERDINGHE to PROVEN. On arrival Bn marched to Camp at P.5.	
	29-10-17		While in camp Refitting and Training carried out.	
PROVEN	30-10-17	6.30 a.m.	Bn moved by train from PROVEN to De WIPPE CAMP.	
			Strength of Bn on 1-10-17 40 Officers 1057 Other Ranks.	
			do do 31-10-17 36 " 935 " "	
			Reinforcements received.	
			3-10-17 — 32 F.R. — 2.O 2.3.3 (Roberts)	
			30-10-17 — " — 11 do.	
			31-10-17 — " — 35 do.	
			Maj. A. H. Munro — 4-10-17 Rd. Base Depot	
			2/Lt. J. McMann — 7-10-17 do.	
			Lt. A.L. Cameron — 7-10-17 do.	
			2/Lt. W. Dawes } do.	
			" N.S. Bird } 9-10-17	
			" J. Grey }	
			" A.J. Grant }	

McArthur Lt Col
Comdg 17th (Service) Battn. The Royal Scots (Rosebery)

Army Form C. 2118.

17th (S) Bn. ROYAL SCOTS.
WAR DIARY
INTELLIGENCE SUMMARY
(Erase heading not required.)

Instructions regarding War Diaries and Intelligence Summaries are contained in F.S. Regs., Part II. and the Staff Manual respectively. Title pages will be prepared in manuscript.

NOVEMBER 1917.

Place	Date	Hour	Summary of Events and Information	Remarks and references to Appendices
HOUTHULST FOREST	1st Nov.			HONOURS MILITARY MEDALS
	3rd. to 7th.		Battalion relieved 14th. Glosters, 105 Brigade, in the HOUTHULST FOREST SECTOR	No. 21752 Sgt.W. Ramsay
			Battalion was relieved in the line by 6th Bn. Royal Berks. On relief Bn. moved to PLUMSTEAD CAMP P.4 Area, PROVEN. Ordinary Training carried on.	No. 20224 L/C A.Leighton
	8th. to 13th.		Battalion moved to PRIVETT CAMP, P 3 Area, PROVEN, Training carried on.	No.24952 Pte. A. Forrest
	14th.		Battalion moved into Canada Area at No.1 Camp, Siege Camp.	No.38301 Pte. W. Steele
	15th.		Battalion relieved 2/5th London Regt. in Support at KEMPTON PARK with 1 Company in PHEASANT TRENCH.	No. 20199 Pte. W. Davie
	16th.		Battalion relieved 2/1st London Regt. in the Left sub-sector of the POELCAPPELLE SECTOR.	
	18th.		Battalion was relieved by 18th H.L.I. in the line and moved into Support at KEMPTON PARK.	CASUALTIES
	20th. to 27th.		Battalion moved to No.5 Camp, Siege Camp. Ordinary Training and Specialist Training was carried out.	1-11-17. 1 Killed O.R.
	28th		Battalion relieved 15th Sherwoods, 105 Inf Bde. in the Left sub-sector of the POELCAPPELLE SECTOR	2-11-17 2 O.Rs. Wounded
	30th.		Battalion was relieved by 4th. N. Stafford Regt. in the line and moved to Support at KEMPTON PARK.	3-11-17 1 O.R. do
			Strength of Bn. at 1-11-17. - 26 Officers 658 O.Rs.	17-11-17
			" at 30-11-17 = 38 " 866 "	2/Lt. J.V. Wilson Killed
			Officers joined Bn.	4 O.Rs. do
			Lt. W.H. Gray, 2/Lts. J. Sim, S. Sinclair, J.V. Wilson. - 9-11-17	12 " Wounded
			2/Lieut. C.A. Petheridge - 10-11-17	
			Casualties (Contd) = 18-11-17 = 14 O.Rs. Wounded, 7 O.Rs. Killed : 19-11-17 1 O.R Wounded	
			20-11-17 - 2 O.Rs. do. : 29-11-17 - 3 O.Rs. Killed, 3 O.Rs. Wounded	
			30-11-17 = 3 " do.	

A. Young
Major.
A/Comdg. 17th. Royal Scots.

1/7 (S) Bn THE ROYAL SCOTS.

WAR DIARY

INTELLIGENCE SUMMARY.

1st December to 31st December 1917

Page 1.

Place	Date	Hour	Summary of Events and Information	Remarks and references to Appendices
				YK 23
near PILKEM	1st		Battn in Bde support in KEMPTON PARK near PILKEM.	Reference
" ELVER-DINGHE	2nd		Battn moved to "E" camp at DIRTY BUCKET CORNER near ELVERDINGHE. Relieved by 17th Lancashire Fusiliers	map 1/20000 sheets 26 NW and 27 N.E.
do	2~			
do	5th		Battn in "E" camp. Training carried out.	Harman & others
near WOESTEN	5th		Battn marched to DRAGON camp between POPERINGHE and WOESTEN	Mention in Dispatch
do	5th		Battn in DRAGON camp carried out training	81668 REM HEATH-COTE.
near WATOU	11th		Battn marched to ROAD camp between POPERINGHE and WATOU.	40552 Sgt J KEOGH
"	11th - 31st		Battn in ROAD camp carried on training, sports etc.	22445 Sgt IT McGrath N I E
near YPRES	21st		Working party of 350 proceeded by train to MURAT camp between BRIELE and YPRES. Battn H.Q. and details remained at ROAD camp.	
	21st		Working parties supplied to R.E. for work on roads, carrying etc in vicinity of LANGEMARCK. Details continued training etc in ROAD camp	

17th (S) Bn THE ROYAL SCOTS

WAR DIARY or INTELLIGENCE SUMMARY.

1st December to 31st December 1917

Page 2

Place	Date	Hour	Summary of Events and Information	Remarks and references to Appendices
near WATOU	27th		Working parties rejoined details in ROADS camp.	
			Strength of Bn at 1/12/17 36 off. 826 o.r.	
			" " " 31/12/17 40 " 879 "	
			Casualties :- nil	
			Reinforcements :- 2/12/17 from R.S. Base depot 2 o.r.	
			23/12/17 do 10 "	
			20/12/17 do Capt W. Simpson	
			31/12/17 do 2/Lt A.A. Kaufmann	
			2/Lt H. Jarvis	
			2/Lt G.A. Murray	

W.J. Wheatley Lt Col
commanding 17th Royal Scots

1/7th (S) Bn THE ROYAL SCOTS   Army Form C. 2118.

WAR DIARY for JANUARY 1918

INTELLIGENCE SUMMARY.
(Erase heading not required.)

Page 2.

Place	Date	Hour	Summary of Events and Information	Remarks and references to Appendices
front line near POELCAPELLE	25th		Battn relieved 18th Bn H.L.I. in front line. 2 coys in line, 1 coy in support at BURNS Ho., 1 coy in reserve at WINCHESTER FM., Bn HQ at HUBNER FM. Boundaries of Battn front LEKKERBOTTERBEEK on left, PADDEBEEK on right.	Casualties 27/1/18 1 or. W. (general) 1 or. K.
do	25th to 29th		Battn in line. Patrols and work on defences carried out.	28/1/18 1 or. W. 29/1/18 1 or. W. 30/1/18 2 or. W.
WIELTJE	29th		Battn were relieved by 19th Bn D.L.I. and moved back to Bde reserve in CALIFORNIA DUGOUTS near WIELTJE.	
do	29th to 31st		Battn in CALIFORNIA DUGOUTS. Working parties supplied to R.E. and improvement of billets carried out.	

Reinforcements:—
25/1/18 2/Lieut L. Hamlet, 2/Lieut A.J.S. Johnston.
3/1/18   1 or. Scottl. B.D.   22/1/18 3 or. Scottl. B.D.
5/1/18   5   "   "   25/1/18 4   "   "
7/1/18   7   "   "

Bn. Strength 1/1/18 33 off. 67# 9 or.
             "   31/1/18 40 " 905 "

H.W.W. Blackadder Lt Col
Comdg 1/7th Royal Scots

2nd M(s)Bn THE ROYAL SCOTS.

WAR DIARY for JANUARY 1918

INTELLIGENCE SUMMARY.
(Erase heading not required.)

Army Form C. 2118.

Place	Date	Hour	Summary of Events and Information	Remarks and references to Appendices
near WATOU	1st to 8th		The Battn carried out training in ROAD CAMP between POPERINGHE and WATOU. Divl. Assault at Arms held on 2nd, 3rd and 4th.	Casualties 14/1/18 1 or. wounded.
near YPRES	8th		The 106th Bde moved into Divl support in the POELCAPELLE sector the Battn proceeding by rail from ROAD CAMP to CANAL BANK near YPRES.	
do	8th to 16th		Battn in CANAL BANK supplied working parties in the forward area.	
ELVERDINGHE	16th		106th Bde moved back into Divl reserve the Battn proceeding by road to BRIDGE CAMP No 2 near ELVERDINGHE.	
do	16th to 21st		Battn in BRIDGE CAMP No 2.	
ST.JULIEN	21st		106th Bde moved into the line, the Battn going into support in the Corps line, east of ST JULIEN with Battn H.Q. and one coy on the banks of the river STEENBEEK near HUGEL HALLE's west of ST JULIEN, taking over from the 13th Bn R.SUSSEX R.	
do	21st to 25th		Battn in Bde support in Corps line. Working and ration carrying parties supplied to front line Battn.	

WAR DIARY or INTELLIGENCE SUMMARY

17th (S). Bn. The Royal Scots for February 1918

Army Form C. 2118.

Place	Date	Hour	Summary of Events and Information	Remarks and references to Appendices
near WIELTJE	1st - 4th		Bn. in CALIFORNIA DUGOUTS near WIELTJE in Bde support. Working parties etc carried out.	Casualties 5/2/18 1 or killed 1 " wounded
near POELCAPELLE	4th		Bn relieved 18th H.L.I. in the front line near POELCAPELLE - Left boundary the LEKKERBOTTERBEEK, right boundary the PADDEBEEK.	6/2/18 1 or killed 5 " wounded
	4th - 8th		In line near POELCAPELLE.	7/2/18 1 or d. of w.
ELVERDINGHE	8th		Bn relieved by 1st Northamptonshire Regt. and moved by train to BRIDGE CAMP No 2 near ELVERDINGHE.	16/2/18 1 or wounded (51.)
do	8th - 16th		Bn in Divl reserve at ELVERDINGHE. Training etc carried out.	18/2/18 4 or. wounded
LANGEMARCK	16th		Bn relieved the 17th Lancs. Fus. in Bde support sector. HQ. Pig and Whistle on LANGEMARCK - PILCKEM Road, 2 coys in LANGEMARCK, 1 coy in BEAR TR. between SCHREIBOOM and KOEKUIT and 1 coy in KOEKUIT and GRUYTERSZALE FM.	21/2/18 1 or. wounded 23/2/18 1 or. d. of w. Honours and awards "Belgian Croix de Guerre" Sergt. J. GORDON 22445 Sgt. T. McGINNEY
do	16th - 18th		Bn in Bde support near LANGEMARCK.	

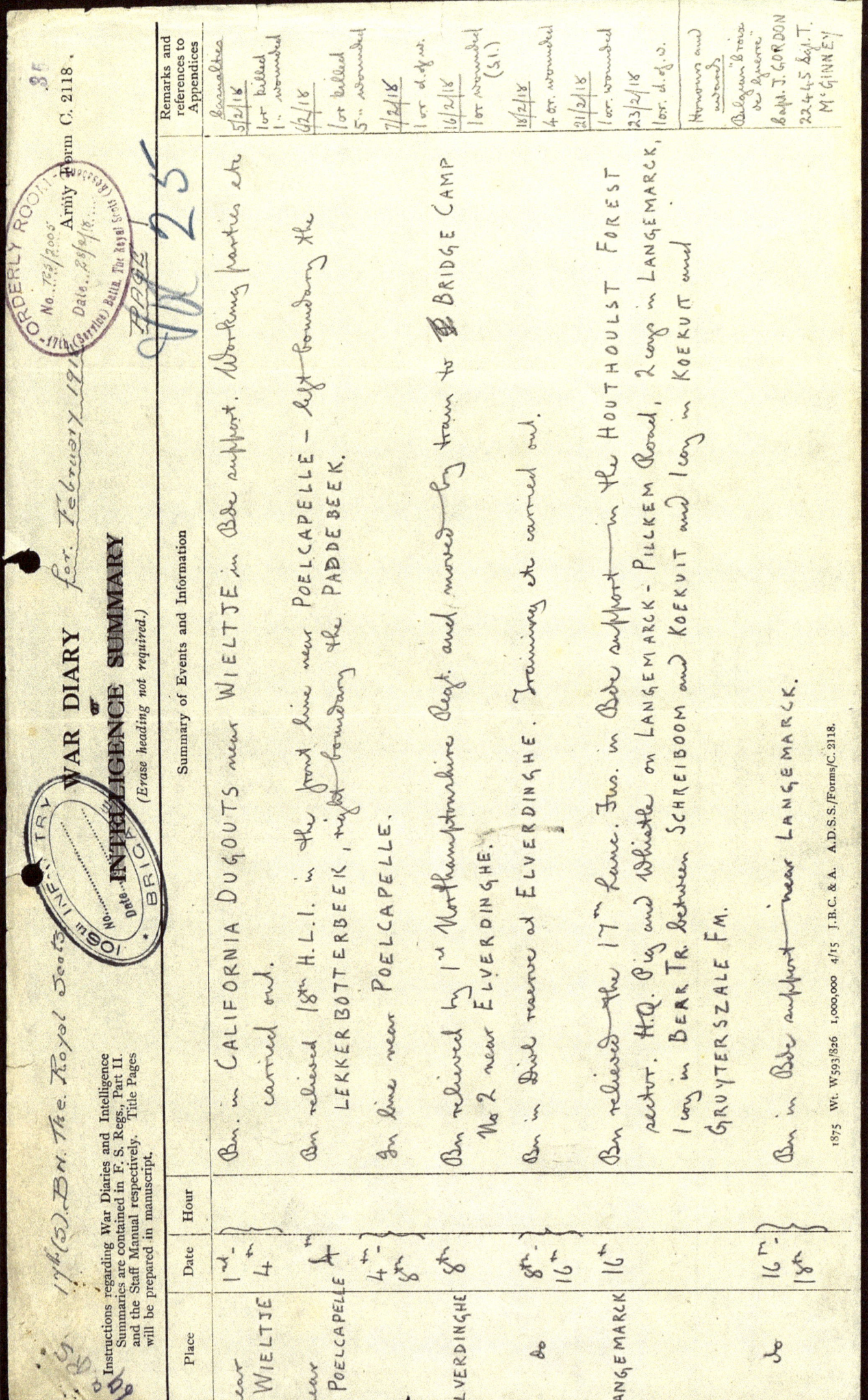

17th (S) Bn The Argyll Suth.

WAR DIARY for February 1918

INTELLIGENCE SUMMARY.

Page 2.

Army Form C. 2118.

Place	Date	Hour	Summary of Events and Information	Remarks and references to Appendices
HOUTHOULST FOREST	18th		Bn relieved 18th H.L.I. in front line near HOUTHOULST FOREST, Bn HQ PASCAL FM. left boundary COLOMBO Ho, right boundary about 100 yds S. of YPRES - STADEN Railway. 2 coys in line, 1 in support and 1 in reserve.	
do	18-22		Bn in line at HOUTHOULST FOREST.	
near PILKEM	22		Bn was relieved by 15th Cheshire R. and moved back to Divl. support - Bn H.Q. and 2 coys KEMPTON PARK, 1 coy GOURNIER FM, 1 coy CADDIE DUGOUTS between PILKEM and YSER CANAL.	
do	22-28		Bn in Divl. support as above carried out work on Army line and wire.	
			Strengths 1st Feb. 39 off. 898 o.r. Draft Lieut. S.W. MITCHELL from Base 25/2/18
			28th - 37 " 960 " 6 o.r. " " 3/2/18
			77 " " " 26/2/18

A. Moyne
[signature] 17th R. Scots

106th Inf.Bde.
35th Div.

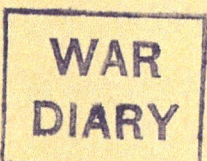

17th BATTN. THE ROYAL SCOTS.

M A R C H

1 9 1 8

17th (S) Bn. The Royal Scots

WAR DIARY for March 1918

INTELLIGENCE SUMMARY.

(Erase heading not required.)

Reference Map 1/40000 Sheet 28
Page I.

Army Form C. 2118.

Place	Date	Hour	Summary of Events and Information	Remarks and references to Appendices
ELVERDINGHE	1st		Battn was relieved in Dirk reserve in Kempton Park by 15th Sherlins R. and moved into Corps reserve in Bridge Camp No 2, ELVERDINGHE.	Casualties 7/3/18 Wounded 1 o.r.
do	1st to 7th		Battn in Bridge Camp. Training, sports etc carried out.	8/3/18 (returned) 1 o.r.
HOUTHOULST FOREST	7th to 9th		Battn went into front line near Houthulst Forest; N boundary Colombo House, S boundary R Broenbeek; 2 coys in front line, 1 coy in support at Egypt House and 1 coy in reserve at Vee Bend; Battn H.Q. Pascal Farm. Patrolling and work on defences etc continued.	9/3/18 Wounded 1 o.r. 23/3/18 to 30/3/18 Killed 30 o.r.
near POPERIN-GHE.	9th		35th Divn was withdrawn from the line into G.H.Q. reserve. The Battn was relieved by 11th Bn Border R, and proceeded by train to Dragon Camp in the Vow Vie Area N.W. of Poperinghe.	Wounded 155 o.r. Missing believed wounded 13 o.r.
do	9th to 16th		Battn in Dragon Camp carried out training, sports, competitions etc.	Missing believed wounded 12 o.r.
do	16th to 21st		Battn in Dragon Camp supplied working parties to Army Battle Zone; parties proceeding to scene of work by train leaving camp at 6 am and returning about 4 pm. Practice of teams for various Divisional competitions continued.	Prisoner 1 o.r.

17th (S) Bn The Royal Scots

WAR DIARY for March 1918

INTELLIGENCE SUMMARY

Army Form C. 2118.

Reference Maps: 1/40000 ALBERT (continued overleaf)

Page II

Place	Date	Hour	Summary of Events and Information	Remarks and references to Appendices
near Dopringhe	22nd		Working parties were continued and training was continued with. Orders received that 35th Divn would be prepared to entrain commencing 17 midnight 22nd/23rd March.	Minnies & Release stragglers 16 or
PROVEN	23rd	7.30 am	Battn entrained.	Killed 27/3/18 Lieut F.A. RAYNES
HEILLY		7 pm	Battn detrained and, less 1 coy, marched to Bray-sur-Somme. 1 coy left at Heilly as Bde unloading party.	M.C.
BRAY-sur-SOMME	23rd/24th	12 midnight	2 coys ordered forward to take up a defensive position round Laphy.	Killed 28/3/18 2/Lt A. CURRIE
	24th	2 am	As many troops as possible required in Maricourt.	Lt M.S. BARCLAY Wounded 24/3/18
MARICOURT		5 am	3 coys on road to Maricourt.	Capt N.B. GRAHAM M.C., R.A.M.C.
do		8 am	Battn in Maricourt.	
do		10 am	Battn ordered to be prepared to take over Bde sector in H5.	Wounded 29/3/18 2/Lt N.J. BIRD
do		2 pm	Battn ordered to assemble in B25d and to be prepared to counterattack.	
near HEM		2.30 pm	Orders received that Battn is at the disposal of G.O.C. 105th Inf Bde and required in H3w at once.	
do		4 pm	Battn took up a defensive position H9a - H3w to which the front line was ordered to withdraw at dusk.	

17th (S) Bn. The Royal Scots

WAR DIARY for March 1916

INTELLIGENCE SUMMARY.
(Erase heading not required.)

Army Form C. 2118.

Page 3.

Place	Date	Hour	Summary of Events and Information	Remarks and references to Appendices
CURLU	24th	5pm	Bde ordered to withdraw front line from H9a - H3a to line Suzanne-Hardecourt-aux-Bois, Bn to be in support immediately behind that line.	
		10pm	On arrival at X roads A30 b 75. 15th Cheshire R. were so weak that Bn was required to occupy front line on road Suzanne - X roads A30 b.	
do	25th	4am	Heavy shelling of A30 by the enemy. Many casualties in sunken road.	
MARICOURT		10am	Left flank forced back, withdrawal towards Maricourt carried out and line taken up running roughly A29 c 57 - A23 d 05.	
do		11pm	Relief of Battn by 2 coys of 17th Lanc. Fus. completed. Battn proceeded to trenches in A22c. On arrival there orders were received to march to Bray-sur-Somme.	
BRAY-sur-SOMME.	26th	2am	Battn arrived in Bray and took up a defensive line on the Albert-Bray road in L2.	
do		12 noon	Enemy reported advancing from Maricourt.	
do		2pm	Enemy in occupation of Bray.	
do		4pm	Battn ordered to retire across the R. Ancre through Morlancourt and Ville-sur-Ancre	
MORLANCOURT		5:30pm	Battn arrived in Morlancourt and was detailed to act as rearguard until	

17th (S) Bn. The Royal Scots

WAR DIARY for March 1918

INTELLIGENCE SUMMARY.
(Erase heading not required.)

Army Form C. 2118.

Page 4.

Place	Date	Hour	Summary of Events and Information	Remarks and references to Appendices
BUIRE-sur-L'ANCRE		7pm	all troops passing through were clear. Village cleared and enemy reported advancing from S and E. Rearguard withdrew and R.Ancre was crossed. Enemy did not follow up for some time.	
		9pm	Batt. arrived in Divl. reserve in road D24 c a and thence proceeded to Laviéville arriving about midnight	
LAVIEVILLE	27	10am	Batt. ordered to be in readiness to relieve 4th N.Staffs in front line from E19c60 to E20a95	
		11am	Relief order issued. Enemy reported to be in E8 & 9 and to be moving in E2. Orders issued to move towards Dernancourt, if possible to relieve front line, if not, to reinforce and establish line. On arr. to move in direction of Buire. Wm. O'Meara to help clean up situation there.	
near DERNANCOURT		2pm	2 coys v H.Q. arrived in line and relieved 4th N.Staffs. 1 coy moving to Buire remaining at road D18 c Situation normal	
		9pm	1 coy which had been acting as Bde. unloading party at Heilly on 23rd and had since then been detached rejoined.	

Army Form C. 2118.

1/7th (S) Bn The Royal Scots

WAR DIARY for March 1918

INTELLIGENCE SUMMARY.
(Erase heading not required.)

Page 5

Place	Date	Hour	Summary of Events and Information	Remarks and references to Appendices
near DERNANCOURT	28th	8am	Enemy reported to be massing reinforcements and to be in occupation of Dernancourt. Battn front quiet.	
		3pm	Heavy casualties by enemy shelling of front.	
		5pm	Situation normal but owing to signs of hostile attack in Buire, coy from D Coy ordered to reinforce, 2 Platoons to front line and 2 platoons to Buire in C.C.S. about E.19 central.	
to	29th	10pm	Arrival of above coy.	
			Quiet day.	
near BUIRE-sur-l'ANCRE		10pm	Battn relieved by 19th D.L.I. and proceeded to bivouac about D24 a 38 in Divl reserve.	
	30th		Battn remaining at D24 a	
		6pm	Relief of 35th Divn by Anzac.	
		10pm	Battn arrived in billets in Heilly.	
HEILLY	31st		In Heilly. Refitting, reorganising etc commenced.	
			Strength 1/3/18 Strength 31/3/16 Increase 54 o.r. from Base 3/3/18. 1 o.r. from Base	
			37 off. 964 o.r. 31 off. 753 o.r. 7/3/18. 2 o.r. from Base 12/3/18. 4 o.r. from Base 19/3/16	

17th (S) Bn. The Royal Scots

WAR DIARY for April 1918
INTELLIGENCE SUMMARY
Army Form C. 2118.

Place	Date	Hour	Summary of Events and Information	Remarks and references to Appendices
HEILLY	1st/4th/5th		Batt. in billets in HEILLY. Training etc carried on.	
BAIZIEUX			Batt. marched to trenches between BAIZIEUX and BRESLE into support of 4th Australian Divn. Dumping packs & blankets at FRANVILLERS. Arrived in position about 2 a.m.	Honours & Awards 11/4/18 M.M. 13077 Pte. J. M'Kendrick
MARTINSART	6th		Batt. returned to FRANVILLERS to collect packs and blankets and marched via WARLOY - HEDAUVILLE - ENGLEBELMER to front line near MARTINSART in relief of units of 47th Divn. Relief completed by 4.15 a.m.	40526 R/c J. Ferguson 40552 Sgt. J. Keogh
do	6th/11th		Batt. in front line on railway embankment between MARTINSART and AVELUY WOOD. Patrolling, work on defences etc carried on during tour.	39342 Pte. E. Lodbell 40866 L/sgt T. Simpson
HEDAUVILLE	11th		Batt. relieved by 18th Lanc. Fus. and, on relief, marched into Divl. reserve in HEDAUVILLE.	40529 Pte. J. Dorman
	12th/14th		Batt. in billets in HEDAUVILLE. Large re-inforcements joined and re-organisation of Batt. commenced.	
BOUZINCOURT	15th		Batt. relieved 4th N. Staff. R. in front line between BOUZINCOURT and AVELUY.	
	15th/16th		Batt. in line nr near BOUZINCOURT. Patrolling, work on defences etc carried on.	
	16/18		Batt. in Bde support in sunken road immediately N. of BOUZINCOURT.	
	18th/20th		Batt. in line near BOUZINCOURT.	
HEDAUVILLE	20th		Batt. relieved by 18th Lanc. Fus. and, on relief, marched back into Divl. Reserve in camp	

"17"(S)Bn The Royal Scots

Army Form C. 2118.

WAR DIARY for April 1918

INTELLIGENCE SUMMARY

(Erase heading not required.)

Page 2

Place	Date	Hour	Summary of Events and Information	Remarks and references to Appendices
HEDAUVILLE	20/22/23ʳᵈ		in valley N. of HEDAUVILLE.	Casualties
MARTINSART	23ʳᵈ		In Div. reserve near HEDAUVILLE. Cleaning and refitting carried out. Batt. relieved 15ᵗʰ Cheshire R. in front line near MARTINSART. Relief completed by 12.15 am 24ᵗʰ	Killed 27/4/18 2/Lt J. WATSON 9/4/18 3 O.R. 24/4/18 2 O.R. 25/4/18 2 " 27/4/18 1 "
	23ʳᵈ/24ᵗʰ		Batt. in line between MARTINSART, AVELUY WOOD.	
	27ᵗʰ	12.30pm	Operation, with it objective the capture of an enemy M.G. strong point on W. edge of AVELUY WOOD, planned. A 6" how bombarded this post deliberately from 12.30pm to 8.45pm, while Divl. artillery & medium T.M.s paid attention to other parts of the Wood.	Died of wounds 9/4/18 1 O.R.
		8.45pm		Wounded
		8.35pm	Enemy put down heavy barrage in valley between our front line and MARTINSART and opened intense M.G. fire from W. edge of AVELUY WOOD.	9/4/18 7 O.R. 16/4/18 3 " 18/4/18 1 "
		8.40pm	SOS sent up on front of Batt. on left.	
		9.15pm	Operation cancelled owing to intensity of M.G. fire, from had to be attacked and remainder of Wood, which swept our parapet and made it impossible for our attacking party to leave the trench.	20/4/18 2 " 19/4/18 1 " 24/4/18 2 " 25/4/18 1 "
		9.45pm	Situation resumed normal.	
HEDAUVILLE	29ᵗʰ		Batt. relieved in front line by 18ᵗʰ Kings Liv and in relief marched back to Div reserve in valley N. of HEDAUVILLE	
RUBEMPRÉ	30ᵗʰ		In Div. reserve near HEDAUVILLE until 30ᵗʰ when Bn. in relief marched to camp & billets	

Army Form C. 2118.

"17th (S) Bn. The Royal Scots

WAR DIARY for April 1918

or INTELLIGENCE SUMMARY.

(Erase heading not required.)

Page 3.

Instructions regarding War Diaries and Intelligence Summaries are contained in F. S. Regs., Part II. and the Staff Manual respectively. Title pages will be prepared in manuscript.

Place	Date	Hour	Summary of Events and Information	Remarks and references to Appendices
RUBEMPRE	30th		in RUBEMPRE arriving about 7 p.m.	26/4/18 1 off
				21/4/18 2 "
			On strength	17/4/18 1 "
			1/4/18 32 officers 832 other ranks	
			30/4/18 35 " 944 "	
			Re-inforcements	
			7/4/18 88 other ranks from Base	22/3/18 4 "
			9/4/18 64 " " "	25/4/18 1 "
			11/4/18 69 " " "	26/4/18 2 "
			15/4/18 10 " " "	28/4/18 1"(S)
			19/4/18 3 " " "	27/4/18 9 "
				29/4/18 2 "
			Officers re-inforcements	
			5/4/18 Major A.L. Scougal, M.C. from Base 24/4/18 2/Lt H.J.S. Lowdens from Base	
			" Lieut. S. McKnight " " " C. Williamson " "	
			22/4/18 2/Lt C.J. Byln " " 29/4/18 " M.T. Hedley " " (to	
			" " W. Bollock " " Corps Re-inforcement Camp.	
			" " S. Kennedy " "	
			" " A.L. Robinson " "	

W.Wheatherhead Lt. Col
comdg 17th R. Scots.

9.1/4(0) Bn The Royal Scots

WAR DIARY for May 1918.

Army Form C. 2118.

Instructions regarding War Diaries and Intelligence Summaries are contained in F. S. Regs., Part II. and the Staff Manual respectively. Title pages will be prepared in manuscript.

INTELLIGENCE SUMMARY
(Erase heading not required)

Place	Date	Hour	Summary of Events and Information	Remarks and references to Appendices
RUBEMPRE	MAY 1st		Bn marched from HEDAUVILLE to RUBEMPRE into Corps Reserve. In Camp at RUBEMPRE. Daily training.	Casualties Killed
	11th		Bn moved to Camp in V.7.b.1.d for trench digging in PURPLE SYSTEM under R.E.	19.5.18: 2 O.R.
near WARLOY	13th		Bn returned to RUBEMPRE + continued training.	20.5.18: 1 "
RUBEMPRE	19th		Bn relieved 14th Bn R.W.F. in AVELUY CENTRE Sector. Quiet tour on the whole.	22.5.18: 2 "
	21st		Bn relieved by 4th Bn N STAFF Regt. moved to Bde Support at V.5.B. 1 Coy remained in PURPLE SYSTEM	26.5.18: 3 "
IN LINE	25th		Bn moved into Support in AVELUY LEFT Sector in PURPLE SYSTEM. Nightworking parties in AVELUY WOOD & PURPLE SYSTEM	Wounded
	29th		Bn moved relieved by 18th LANC. FUS. & moved to Camp in Bde Reserve at P.33.B. 1 Coy left in PURPLE "	LT. S. SINCLAIR on 18.6.18: 1 O.R.
				16.5.18: 1 O.R.
			During period in Reserve at RUBEMPRE Musketry was principle feature in training, also absorption of recent reinforcements and organisation of Platoons. A new organisation of Bde Lewis Gun Platoon	19.5.18: 9 "
			at Bn HQ and one L.G. Platoon in each of W+Y Coys was commenced carried out.	24.5.18: 10 "
			On 16th May the Bn won competition for best turned out Transport in 35th Division.	26.5.18: 10 "
			" 17 " " " " " " inter. platoon Rapid fire competition open to 35th Division.	28.5.18: 1 "
				29.5.18: 1 "
			During tour in the line enemy artillery was active but gas shelling by enemy increased in frequency and intensity. There were no infantry actions.	31.5.18: 2 "

Officer Reinforcements 6.5.18. 2/Lt A. WOOD from Base
14.5.18 " J. MOYES " "
" C.E. FEATHERSTON " "
" J.G. SCOTT " "

MENTIONED IN DESPATCHES (23.5.18) LT-COL R.E.M. HEATHCOTE, CAPT. W.R. DUFF, LIEUT M.S. BARCLAY

STRENGTH OF BN.
1.5.18   35 Officers   950 O.Rs
31.5.18 36   "   881   "

Alex G. Seniger
Lt Col
17th R Scots

Army Form C. 2118.

WAR DIARY for June 1918.

17th. (S) Bn. The Royal Scots.

Instructions regarding War Diaries and Intelligence Summaries are contained in F.S. Regs., Part II. and the Staff Manual respectively. Title pages will be prepared in manuscript.

(Erase heading not required.)

Place	Date	Hour	Summary of Events and Information	Remarks and references to Appendices
MARTINSSART	1st. to 16th.		The Bn. relieved Durh. L.I. on the Right Battalion Front of the AVELUY Left Sub-sector	Honours & Awards. D.S.O. Lt. Col. R.E.M. Heathcote
	16th.		The Battalion in line in the AVELUY LEFT SUB-SECTOR. Active patrolling and work on Defences carried out	
	16th.		The Battalion relieved by 6th. Queens' Regt. and marched to WARLOY, billeting there overnight 16th./17th.	
WARLOY	17th		Battalion marched to RAINCHEVAL and 35th. Division came into G.H.Q. Reserve.	M.S.M. 24974 L/C J. Brandie
RAINCHEVAL	17th to 30th.		Battalion in RAINCHEVAL. Training, sports, musketry competitions &c. carried out.	
			Casualties.	
			Strength 1/6/18 Off 920 O.Rs.	
			" 30-6-18 38 Off 920 O.Rs.	
			Drafts. Capt. C.S. Matley -15-6-18.	
			Lieut. C.J.F.Robison - 5-6-18.	
			2/Lt. C. Mann - 24-6-18	
			" R.A. Wyllie)	
			Not yet (2/Lt. A. Wilson) - 28-6-18.	
			joined Bn. (" H.M.Johnston)	
			9 O.Rs. from Base - 10-6-18.	
			28 " " " - 11-6-18.	
			10 " " " - 17-6-18.	
			19 " " " - 26-6-18.	
			16 " " " - 27-6-18	

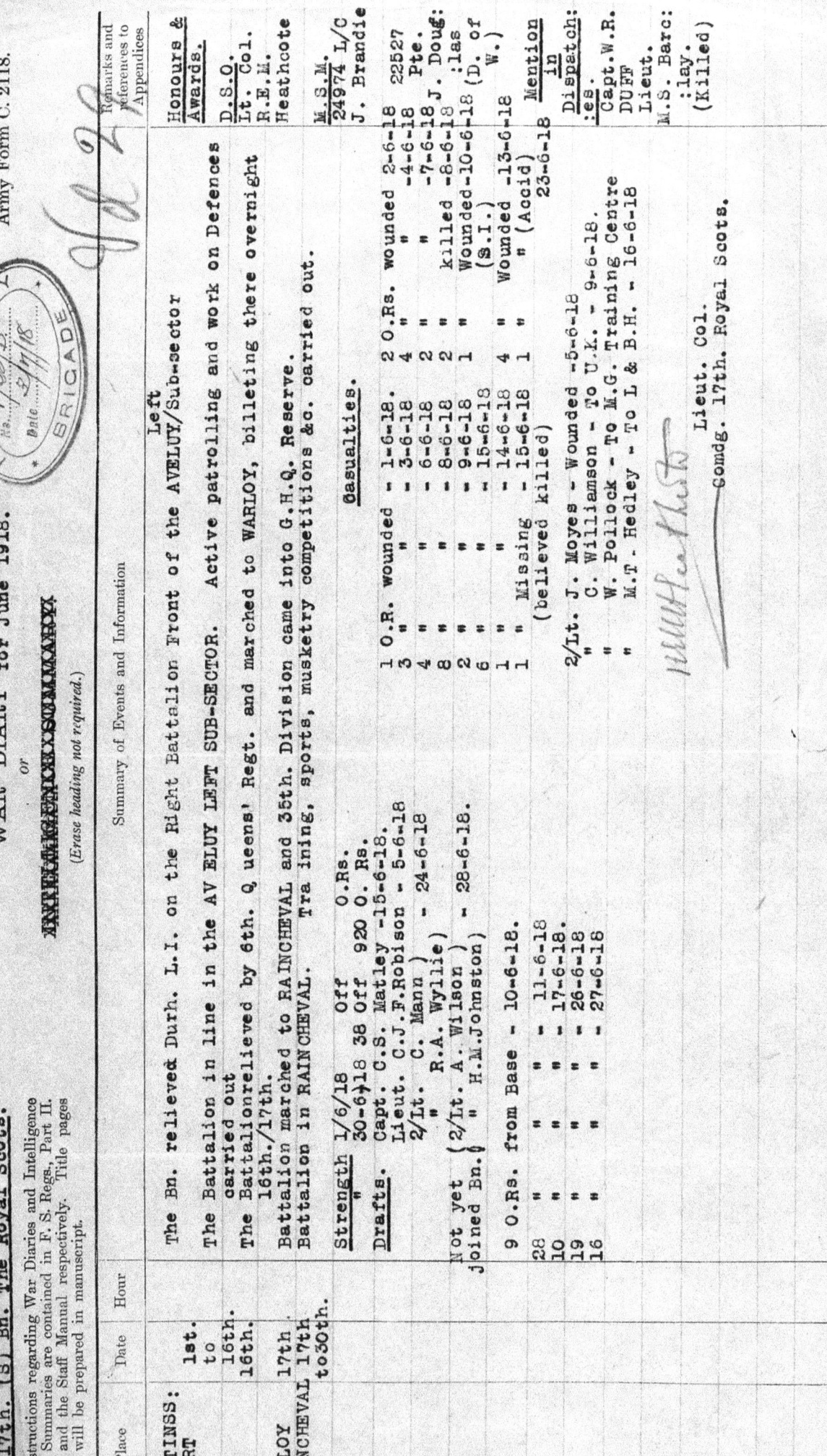

Casualties.

1 O.R. wounded - 1-6-18   2 O.Rs. wounded 2-6-18
3 "   "   - 3-6-18   4   "   "   -4-6-18 22527
4 "   "   - 6-6-18   2   "   "   -7-6-18 Pte.
8 "   "   - 8-6-18   2   "   killed -8-6-18 J. Doug:
2 "   "   - 9-6-18   1   "   Wounded-10-6-18 :las
6 "   "   -15-6-18   (S.I.)   (D. of
1 "   "   -14-6-18   4   "   Wounded -13-6-18   W.)
1 "   Missing -15-6-18   1   "   "   (Accid)
         (believed killed)   23-6-18

2/Lt. J. Moyes - Wounded -5-6-18
 "   C. Williamson - To U.K.- 9-6-18.
 "   W. Pollock - To M.G. Training Centre
 "   M.T.- Hedley - To L & B.H. - 16-6-18

Mention in Dispatch: :es.
Capt.W.R. DUFF
Lieut.
M.S. Barc: :lay.
(Killed)

M.W.Heathcote
Lieut. Col.
Comdg. 17th. Royal Scots.

17 Royal Scots Army Form C. 2118.

WAR DIARY

~~INTELLIGENCE SUMMARY~~

(Erase heading not required.)

JULY 1918. 17th (Service) Battn. The Royal Scots

Instructions regarding War Diaries and Intelligence Summaries are contained in F.S. Regs., Part II. and the Staff Manual respectively. Title pages will be prepared in manuscript.

Place	Date	Hour	Summary of Events and Information	Remarks and references to Appendices
DOULLENS	1st.		Battalion moved by train from DOULLENS to ARQUES and thence by road to LE NIEPPE. Billetted there for night 1st/2nd. inst.	
LE NIEPPE	2nd.		Battalion moved by bus to ZERMEZEELE and billeted there for the night 2nd./3rd.	
ZERMEZEELE	3rd.		Battalion moved by Route March to ST. LAURENT and billeted there for the night 3rd/4th. and 4th./5th.	
ST. LAURENT	5th.-10th.		Battalion relieved 6th. Battalion of the 221st. French Division in the Support System of the Right Sub-sector of the LOCRE Sector.	
TRENCHES	Night 10/11th. - 16th.		Battalion relieved 18th.High. L.I. in the Right Battalion Front Line System of the LOCRE Sector.	
	16/17th.		Battalion less two Coys. relieved by 12th. High. L.I. in Front Line System and moved into Brigade Reserve.	
	17/18th.		Two Coys. relieved in Front Line System and rejoined the Battalion in Brigade Reserve.	
	22nd.		Battalion relieved 18th. High. L.I. in Support System of the Right Sub-sector of the LOCRE Sector	
	Night 22nd./23rd			
	Night 25th/26th.		Battalion relieved by 2/15th. London Regt. 90th. Brigade, 30th. Division, and moved to EECKE to prepare for Operations to be carried out by the 106th. Infantry Brigade in the LOCRE Sector.	
	26th.-31st.		Battalion carred out training inconnection with operations	

Strength of Battalion as at 1-7-18.- 38 Offrs. 920 O.Rs.
Strength of Battalion as at 31-7-18.- 39 " 918 "

Casualties
2nd. Lieut. A.G. Robinson Pronounced "B.1" - 2-7-18.
2nd. Lieut. A. Wilson Killed in action - 16-7-18. Lieut. J.R. Haddow } To 106th. T.M.B
Lieut. J. Deuchars - To M.G. Training Centre - 18-7-18. 2/Lt. C.J. Fynn } Est. 25-7-18.
Lieut. H.F.S. Lowery - To 13th. R. Scots - 23-7-18.

1 O.R.	Wounded -	8-7-18	1 O.R.	Died of Wounds -	9-7-18	1 O.R. Wounded - 9-7-18
2 "	" -	10-7-18	1 "	Wounded -	12-7-18.	2 " Wounded -14-7-18
2 "	Killed -	15-7-18	1 "	Died of Wounds -	15-7-18	3 " " -15-7-18
6 "	" -	16-7-18	2 "	Wounded -	16-7-18	1 " Killed - 17-7-18
5 "	Wounded -	17-7-18	1 "	" -	21-7-18	2 " Wounded - 25-7-18

Army Form C. 2118.

17th. (S) Bn. The Royal Scots.
WAR DIARY (Contd)

~~INTELLIGENCE SUMMARY~~

(Erase heading not required.)

JULY 1918.

Instructions regarding War Diaries and Intelligence Summaries are contained in F. S. Regs., Part II. and the Staff Manual respectively. Title pages will be prepared in manuscript.

Place	Date	Hour	Summary of Events and Information	Remarks and references to Appendices
			Reinforcements.	
			Officers.	
			Lieut. T.G. Stewart M.C. } From Base	
			2/Lt. J.T.E. Storer } 22-7-18	
			Lieut. J. Crawford } From Base	
			2/Lt. P.G. Brentz } 25-7-18	
			2/Lieut. P. Bourhill } From Base	
			2/Lieut. A.S. Asquith } 29-7-18	
			O.Rs.	
			1 O.R. from Base - 6-7-18.	
			20 " " " - 10-7-18.	
			10 " " " - 17-7-18.	
			11 " " " - 22-7-18.	
			20 " " " - 23-7-18	
			12 " " " - 26-7-18.	
			Honours and Awards.	
			- Nil -	
			[signature] Lieut. Col.	
			Comdg. 17th. Royal Scots.	

11th (Service) Battn. The Royal Scots

Army Form C. 2118.

Instructions regarding War Diaries and Intelligence
Summaries are contained in F. S. Regs., Part II.
and the Staff Manual respectively. Title pages
will be prepared in manuscript.

WAR DIARY
or
INTELLIGENCE SUMMARY.
(Erase heading not required.)

Place	Date	Hour	Summary of Events and Information	Remarks and references to Appendices
MONT VIDAIGNE	1st		Bn moved by bus into SUPPORT of the right subsector of the LOCRE SECTOR for prospective operations	
	2nd		Operations postponed owing to weather conditions	
BOESCHEPE	3rd		Bn moved into Bde Reserve of LOCRE SECTOR around BOESCHEPE. LOCRE SECTOR rearranged from one of Three Bde Front to one of Two Bde Front with one Bde in Reserve	
	4th			
MONT VIDAIGNE	5th		Bn moved into SUPPORT (MONT VIDAIGNE) for prospective operations	
	6th		Lt Col R.E.M. HEATHCOTE D.S.O. to U.K. (2 months) Major A.G. Seagal M.C. took over command of Bn	
	7th		Operations cancelled owing to weather conditions. Bn moved into front line and relieved 15th Notts Derby	
	8th			
MONT VIDAIGNE	9th		Bn relieved by 2nd S. LANCS REST and moved to SUPPORT on MONT VIDAIGNE.	
EECKE	10th		Bn relieved by 7/8th INNISKILLIN Fus. in SUPPORT and moved to CORPS RESERVE area EECKE.	
	to 17th		Training carried on	
LEWAST	18th-23rd		Bn moved by train and march route to LEWAST for musketry training	
EECKE	24th		Bn moved back to Corps Reserve area around EECKE. Training carried on	
	30th		Prepared to relieve 9th INNIS KILLIN Fus in ST JANS CAPPEL area. Enemy withdrawal relief cancelled	
	31st		Training carried on	

Army Form C. 2118.

WAR DIARY

~~INTELLIGENCE SUMMARY~~

17th. (S) Bn. The Royal Scots.

(Erase heading not required.)

Instructions regarding War Diaries and Intelligence Summaries are contained in F. S. Regs., Part II. and the Staff Manual respectively. Title pages will be prepared in manuscript.

AUG 1918

Place	Date	Hour	Summary of Events and Information	Remarks and references to Appendices
			Officers Joining.	
			2nd. Lieut. A. Ruston Base 31-7-18	
			2nd. Lieut. E.E. Coney " 8-8-18	
			2nd. Lieut. W.A.I. Forbes " 22-8-18	
			Major C. Anderson M.C. " 28-8-18	
			2nd. Lieut. J.L. Fair " 28-8-18	
			2nd. Lieut. A. Bennie " 28-8-18	
			2nd. Lieut. A.C. Ronaldson " 29-8-18	
			Officers Quitting.	
			Lt. Col. R.E.M. Heath cpts. To U.K. (six months)	5-8-18
			Capt. W.R. Duff D.S.O. do.	2-8-18
			" G.B. Russell M.C. do.	4-8-18
			Lieut. H. Gladstone do.	4-8-18
			Casualties.	
			1 O.R. Wounded - 3-8-18	
			4 " " 6-8-18	
			3 " " 7-8-18	
			3 " " 8-8-18	
			2 " " 9-8-18	
			Drafts.	
			2 O.Rs. Base - 9-8-18	
			1 " " 12-8-18	
			2 " " 8-8-18	
			2 " " 17-8-18	
			1 " " 19-8-18	
			1 " " 28-8-18	
			Honours & Awards.	
			Lieut. H.F.S. Lowery - MILITARY CROSS (now 13th. R. Scots)	
			No. 40934 Pte. J. Watt - DISTIN:GUISED (Wounded) CONDUCT MEDAL	
			No. 59665 Pte. A. Ross) MILITARY	
			40925 " J. Fleming) MEDALS.	
			Strength of Battalion as at 1st. August 1918. - 40 Officers 916 O.Rs.	
			Strength of Battalion as at 31st. August 1918.- 40 Officers 896 O.Rs.	

Major.
Comdg. 17th. Royal Scots.

WAR DIARY
or
INTELLIGENCE SUMMARY.
(Erase heading not required.)

Army Form C. 2118.

1/7th (T) Bn. The R. Scots.

Place	Date	Hour	Summary of Events and Information	Remarks and references to Appendices
STEENVOORDE	1-9-18	–	Bn. in Camps between Locke and Steenvoorde	
	2-9-18	–	Bn. moved by March route to Billets in Road Camp near St Jans cr Biezen	
Trenches	3-9-18	–	Bn. proceeded by Light Railway to Bat. Support in Right Subsector of Canal Sector in relief of 2 Coys. 1st Bn. and 2 Coys 3rd Bn of 119th Regt 30th American Division.	
	6/7-9-18		Bn. relieved 1st Royal Scots in Front Line of Right Subsector Canal Sector	
ERIE Camp	12/13-9-18		Bn. relieved by 15th Sherwood Foresters and moved back to Divisional Reserve near Kamp ERINSHE	
Trenches	17/18-9-18		Bn. relieved 1st Dur. L.I. in Front Line of Left Subsector of Canal Sector	
	20/21		Inter Coy relief carried out within Battalion.	
	22/23		2 Coys relieved by 11th Lanc Fusiliers, 1 in Front Line and 1 in Support, and moved back to Camp near VLAMERTINGHE.	
	24/25, 29/30		Inter Bn. relief carried out within Battalion.	
			Bn. engaged in Active operations. Report attached.	

Strength on 1-9-18 = 36 off. 896 ord.
Strength on 30-9-18 = 23 " 543 "

Casualties: Major P.G. Jeoffrey MC – K in 10.9.18
  " A.J. Mopurk – M in A 18.9.18
Capt. S. McKnight – W in A 24.9.18
  " J.C. CRAIG – K in R 29.9.18
  " N.A. Adams – W – A "
2/Lt At. Tait MC – K – A "
  " J. Kennedy – W – A "
  " R. Fuston – W – A "
  " P.G. Symonn – W – A "
  " P. Bourhill – W – A "
  " L. Hamlet – W – P "
  " A.I. Grant – missing 30.9.18
  " A. Bennie – missing 30.9.18

Book W in A 4.9.18
5 " W. J.W. 5.9.18
3 " W in A 9.9.18
4 " W. J.W. 12.9.18
1 " K in A 12.9.18
1 " W – A 13.9.18
2 " K in A 15.9.18
10 " W – A 16.9.18
1 " W – A 17.9.18
2 " W in A 19.9.18
5 " K in A 22.9.18
8 " W in A 24.9.18
1 " W – A 25.9.18
3 " W – A 25.9.18
1 " W. J.W. 25.9.18
295 " Casualties 28.9.18 – 30.9.18
2 " K in A 27.9.18

Reinforcements
Major C. Anderson MC – 4.9.18
Lieut WO Inman – 7.9.18
3 ors from Base – 23.9.16

[signature] Lieut. Col.
Comdg. 1/7 R. Scots.

17th (S) Bn. The Royal Scots.

REPORT on operations engaged in from 25th September 1918 until 1st October 1918.

During the night 27/28th September at ZILLEBEKE (Canal Sector) the Battalion assembled for attack in reserve to the 12th and 18th Battalions Highland Light Infantry, without incident - one Coy. continuing to hold the front line posts in the vicinity of MANOR FARM (I.22 c.8-4), the remaining three Coys. and Bn.H.Q. being around BELGIAN BATTERY CORNER.

At 5.30 a.m. on the morning of 28th September the attack was launched and at 6.50 a.m. the Battalion moved forward according to order and advanced to second assembly positions immediately S.W. of ZILLEBEKE LAKE.

At 8.45 a.m. the Battalion was ordered forward to take up positions in close support to 12th H.L.I. at HEDGE STREET TUNNELS (I.30.b.5-2) arriving there and taking up positions on the Western slopes of the hill. At 11.45 a.m. the Battalion was ordered to advance and cooperate on the left flank of the 18th H.L.I. in occupying and holding the ALASKA HOUSES RIDGE in J.33.d.

On arrival at this ridge, the 18th H.L.I. were found to be in possession of the crest and I accordingly disposed the Battalion on the left flank of the 18th H.L.I. holding tactical positions to the immediate North of ALASKA HOUSES.

No signs of the Division operating on the left flank having been observed, patrols were sent out on the afternoon of the 28th and morning of the 29th, and in both cases touch was established. about J.36.d.

The Battalion remained in position on ALASKA HOUSES RIDGE until the afternoon of the 29th September when orders were received that the 106th Brigade would advance in support to 105th Brigade on ZANDVOORDE, and thereafter support them in capturing the TENBRIELEN - BLAEGNERT FARM (P.11.d.90-90.) line and pushing on towards WERVICQ, 18th H.L.I. being on the right, 17th The Royal Scots on the left, and 12th H.L.I. in reserve.

This order was later altered, and I was ordered to attack and support the left flank of the N.STAFFS. REGIMENT who were going forward to assist in capturing the above objectives. At 3.10 p.m. the Battalion advaced and passed through ZANDVOORDE without resistance advancing with its right flank on the ZANDVOORDE - TENBRIELEN road. The enemy shelled very vigourously and the Battalion came under very heavy machine gun fire on the forward slope of the hill. The advance was checked, and progress was only possible by cooperation of fire and movement which was very effectively carried out. Progress was necessarily slow until troops, later identified as "C" Coy. 12th H.L.I. were seen advancing from the rightflank on to enemy positions in P.13.d. and P.10.a. At this time the enemy, to an estimated strength of 300, had assembled for counter attack astride the road in P.10.a. and d. I ordered the two leading Coys. (Capt. Craig and Capt. Matley) to push straight on and capture the enemy M.G. positions in front. The enemy still maintained a heavy fire, but owing to the resoluteness and tenacity of the advance, broke and retired. The advance was carried on and as night fell a line from approximately P.10.d.4-0 to P.11.a.4-3. was taken up. Patrols were pushed forward to BLEGNAERT FARM AND TENBRIELEN.

During the night 29th-30th September orders were received that an attack on the Northern outskirts of WERVICQ by the Brigade: 12th and 18th H.L.I. assaulting; 17th The Royal Scots and Cheshires (105th Bde.) in support, would be projected at 6.15 a.m. the following morning.

(2).

The assault Battalions assembled and advanced at 6.15 a.m. passing through the 17th Royal Scots, who followed on in left support to the 18th H.L.I. For the first 1500 yards the advance was without incident, but thereafter heavy machine gun fire was opened in front and on both flanks. This fire from the left flank was seriously hampering the left attack, and in consultation with the O.C. 12th and 18th H.L.I., I pushed forward two Coys. to protect the flank, the remaining two Coys. continuing in support. As the advance progressed towards the village the two Coys. were able to make good ground about Q.19.c.9-2. and the remaining two Coys. moved forwad to cover this position. In order to support and protect the flank, it had been found necessary to cross a deep belt of wire and shortly after reaching the point above mentioned very heavy fire was opened on the Battalion from its exposed flank and from the left rear. Fire was located as coming from certain pill boxes, one of which was rushed, the garrison of 1 N.C.O. and 6 men being taken prisoners. Owing to the nature of the ground and lack of cover, casualties were becoming very heavy and it was impossible to clear the other machine guns out of position. By this nearly all the officers were casualties and the Battalion suffered heavily from the loss of N.C.Os.

Under cover of this heavy machine gun fire, the enemy counter attacked the flank of the support Coys. who were forced out of position. Before evacuating the position every effort was made to cover the withdrawal of the leading two Coys. which by now were of very weak strength. This was effected with the exception of two platoons which owing to their advanced position could not extricate themselves. A line was formed approximately Q.19.c.1-7. to Q.24.b.7-7 supporting the left flank of 18th H.L.I. which was maintained until the Battalion was relieved by the 7th Royal Irish Regiment, 30th Division.

Despite every effort during the day of the 30th, no touch was established with any troops on the left flank.

As a result of the operations the Battalion has suffered casualties amounting to 13 officers and 296 O.Rs. mainly inflicted during the attack on ZANVOORDE and the WERVICQ operations.

The booty, &c., captured amounted to 14 prisoners; three 4.2 guns; and one 77mm. gun; and one machine gun. Other booty cannot be detailed as no time to check and examine same was available.

The services of the attached section A Coy. 35 M.G.Bn. were of great value, and I commend to notice the officer 2/Lieut. Barr, who performed valuable services and was killed in reconnoitring advanced positions in the afternoon of 30th September.

I also commend the services of my Medical Officer (Capt. G. Grant) who although working under great difficulties, was most useful in tending and evacuating the wounded.

The ration arrangements were excellent, and at no time were the men without food or water.

I should also like to bring to notice the action of "C" Coy., 12th Highland Light Infantry in the afternoon of 29th September 1918 during the attack on ZANVOORDE.

The behaviour of all ranks was magnificent. Considering that they had done 12 continuous days in the front line prior to the commencement of operations, I consider that their fighting powers and endurance were beyond description.

Where all ranks have done so well, it is difficult to single out any specific person or deed, but a list of officers N.C.Os. and men who have shewn great gallantry and devotion to duty is forwarded herewith.

C.P. Etherbridge
Capt & adjt
for Lt.- Col.
Comdg. 17th (S) Bn.
The Royal Scots.

3:10:18.

17th The Royal Scots.

Operation Order No.104.

SECRET.

Ref. Sheets 1/10000 YPRES
GHELUVELT & WYTSCHAETE.

24/25th Sept. 1918.

1. On "J" day at "H" hour 106th Inf. Bde in conjunction with ~~other~~ other formations will attack. 87th Inf. Bde. (29th Div.) will be on the left and 104th Inf. Bde. on the right.

2. The objectives of 106th Inf. Bde. will be:-
   (a) First Objective. High ground from CANADA TUNNELS (I 30. a. 80. 25.) exclusive - road through I 30 b. and J 19 c to J 19 a 95. 05 - JAM LANE - I 24 b 90. 60.

   (b) Second Objective. ALASKA HOUSES (J 33 b.)

3. Boundaries of attack of 106th Bde. will be as follows:-
   North:- I 22 d & 2. - N. end of MAPLE COPSE - I 24 b 90. 30.
   South:- Railway in I 22. c inclusive to I 22 c 60.25. - road I 29 a 45.55. - KNOLL FARM (exclusive) - MORLAND AVENUE - CANADA TUNNELS (exclusive) I 30 a 80.25.

4. Units of 106th Bde. will take up assembly positions on night J - 1 day as follows:-
   (a) 12th H.L.I. and 2 guns and carrying party 106th T.M.B. position west of MANOR FARM from I 22 c 35.35. - I 22 c 30.70.
   Bn. H.Q. I 21 c 4.8.
   (b) 18th H.L.I.
       2 Coys. Railway Embankment I 20 a 8.3. - I 20 b 45.05.
       2 Coys. G.H.Q. 1 line I 20 a 0.10. - I 20 a 10.90.
       Bn. H.Q. I 20 d 9.9.
   (c) 17th R. Scots.
       1 Coy holding front line posts to remain in position and cover assembly, attack passing through them.
       3 Coys. in GOLDFISH LINE from DINGO FARM (H 16 a. - H 11 a 95.15.)
       Bn. H.Q. H. 24 b 5.8.

5. The Battalion will move to assembly positions as follows:-
   Y Coy. will remain in front line posts until attack has passed through, and further orders are received from H.Q.
   X Coy. will after 12th H.L.I. have passed G.H.Q. 1 line with-draw to GOLDFISH LINE. Route:- DERBY ROAD - light railway track I 19 b 25.25. - CARTRIDGE - BRISBANE DUMP - H 18 c 85.20. - H 18 c 0.7. - H 17 d 0.7. - H 17 c 25.55. - H 16 d 15.80. - DINGO FARM - GOLDFISH LINE (right).
   W and Z Coys. from billets in H 8a. to GOLDFISH LINE (centre) and (left) respectively as follows:-
       Starting Point.- Road Junction H 8 a 5.3.
       Time. 9.45 p.m. (to follow 18th H.L.I.)
       Order of March:- Z,W.
       Route.- Cross roads H 8 d 7.3. - H 8 d 9.6. - Road Junction
               H 9 a 75.55. - H 9 b 4.2. - DINGO FARM - GOLDFISH LINE
               (Z Coy. to left and W Coy. to centre).

O.C.Coys. will ensure that at least one officer per Coy. and 1 N.C.O. and 2 O.Rs. per platoon are fully conversant with route to Assembly Positions. Reconnaissances, if necessary to be done forthwith.
Coys. (less "Y" Coy.) will report to BN.H.Q. by runner when they are in assembly positions.

(2).

6. The attack will be carried out as follows:-
   12th H.L.I. in front
   18th H.L.I. in support.
   17th R.Scots in reserve

   (a) At "H" hour, 12th H.L.I. will assault and capture the first
   objective. They will maintain liaison with 87th Inf. Bde.
   at north end of APLE COPSE and at I 24 b 90.60. and with
   104 Inf. Bde. at CANADA TUNNELS.

   (b) 18th H.L.I. will be prepared if necessary to support 12th
   H.L.I. in capturing first objective. Should attack proceed
   favourably, 18th H.L.I. will advance from assembly positions
   at "H" plus 1 hour 20 minutes, with 1 platoon Corps Cyclists,
   to line captured by 12th H.L.I. At "H" plus 4 hours 20 minutes
   18th H.L.I. with Cyclists, 1 Sec. 35 Bn. M.G.C., and Field
   Artillery will push forward and secure ALASKA HOUSES (J 33 b.)
   88th Inf. Bde. on left will similarly secure GHELUVELT and
   KRUISEEKE.
   104th Inf.Bde. on right will seize ZANDVOORDE.
   18th H.L.I. will establish combined post with 104th Bde.
   about J 25. central. Touch will be obtained with 88th Bde.
   If possible 18th H.L.I. will continue beyond ALASKA HOUSES.

   (c) 17th Royal Scots. Y Coy. in front line posts will remain in
   position after attack has passed through, and await orders.
   This time will be spent in equipping the Coy.
   At "H" plus 1 hour 20 minutes, the Battalion (less Y Coy.)
   will move forward to assembly positions vacated by 18th
   H.L.I. as follows:-
        W Coy. to railway embankment I 20 a 8.3. - I 20 b 45.05.
        Z Coy. and X Coy. to G.H.Q. 1 line.
        Bn. H.Q. to I 20 d 9.9.
   Route. (Z and X Coys.) Light railway track from SQUARE KEEP
   (H 16 b.) - H 17. c.25.85. - RUPERT (H 17 d.) FRANKTON (H 17 d.)
   - H 18 c 85.20 - BRIGADE DUMP - CARTRIDGE -thence to G.H.Q.
   1 line.
        (W Coy.) As above thence to railway embankment.

   Order of March.
        H.Q., W, Z, X Coys.

   Starting Point
        H 24 b 65.55. (level crossing)
        Five minutes interval between Coys. 50 yards between
   platoons or such other formation as shelling demands. O.C.
   Coys. and Lieut. Gray for H.Q. will take necessary steps to
   reconnoitre this route forthwith. O.C. Coys. (less Y Coy.)
   will report by runner to Bn. H.Q. when they are in their
   new positions.

7. On arrival in positions detailed in para 6., the Battalion will
   remain in Brigade Reserve, prepared to move forward to first
   objective, replacing 18th H.L.I., and thence to move forward in
   support of 18th H.L.I. according to circumstances.

8. Details of Machine Gun and Artillery action have been issued
   verbally to O.C. Coys.

9. (A) A <u>Contact</u> aeroplane (marked by one black flap projecting
   from each lower plane and streamer from tail) will fly along
   the front of attack at about one hour after zero, and thereafter
   every clock hour.
   <u>Front line</u> troops will show their position by lighting flares

(3).

flashing discs, when the aeroplane demands recognition by sounding letter "A" in Morse on Klaxon Horn, or by firing a single white light. Message maps laid on parapet may also be used as communication by front line troops.

(b) A counter attack aeroplane will patrol the front from zero plus 40 minutes onwards and will signal developement of enemy counter attack by firing a "Red Parachute" flare and flying in the direction of the enemy massing to attack.

10. Signalling Officer will arrange to indicate position of Bn.H.Q. by Ground Signal Sheets and strips, and to communicate where necessary by means of POPHAM "T" PANEL.
He will also arrange visual and other communication between Coys. and B.H.Q., and B.H.Q. and Brigade, as the situation demands. He will carry within "V" signal calling for S.A.A. which will be exhibited at Bn.H.Q. as ordered.

11. Prisoners of war will be passed back under escort by Coys. to Bn.H.Q. As small an escort as is consistent with safety will be used. No escort will proceed further back than to the Coy. in its immediate rear. Bn. H.Q. will arrange escorts to convey prisoners to ASSAM FARM N 22 a 2.7.
Prisoners may be utilised to carry wounded back but must on no account be sent forward again to carry more. Such carrying must not unnecessarily delay the sending back of prisoners.

12. Dress and Equipment will be as follows:-
Riflemen.
Fighting Order. 200 rounds S.A.A.
Ground Flares. Aeroplane discs. 2 Bombs.
Lewis Gunners Nos.1.
Fighting Order. Lewis Gun and 1 magazine; revolver and 24 rounds ammunition.
do. do. Nos.2. Fighting Order, rifle and bayonet; 3 magazines; spare parts bag.
Nos. 3, 4 and 5.
As for No.2 but with 4 magazines and no spare parts bag. In addition bombs and aeroplane flares and discs will be carried.
Rifle Grenadiers. (used as such)
As for Riflemen, but with cup attachments and 6 No.23 grenades in haversack. 150 rounds S.A.A.

N.C.Os. will be dressed and equipped exactly as the men.
Officers will wear fighting order.
All ranks will carry one day's rations and Iron Ration and second water bottle.

13. Up to zero Aid Posts will be situated as follows:-

12th and 18th H.L.I.   I 20 b 6.0.
17th Royal Scots   DOLLS HOUSE, I 19. b 2.5.
Advanced Dressing Station   BELGIAN BATTERY CORNER.
Any change in location of R.A.P. will be intimated to Coys.

14. Reports.
Situation and progress reports will be sent to Bn.H.Q. every half hour in addition to any special report. Coys will inform Bn.H.Q. location of Coy. H.Q. as soon as possible, and intimate any change.
Casualty reports will be rendered to B.H.Q. every three hours after zero.

(4).

14. (Contd.)

2/Lieut. Jarvis and scouts will arrange to keep in touch with situation and report.

15. "J" day and "H" hour will be intimated later. Synchronisation of watches will also be arranged later.

16. BnH.q. at H 24 b 5.5. until H plus 1 hour 20 minutes thereafter at I 20 d 9.9.
Any further change of location of Bn.H.q. will be intimated later. If possible an. flag will be erected to guide runners. Bde. H.Q. at I 20 d 75.95. nd will move to HEDGE STREET TUNNELS after first objective has been secured.
Rear Bde.H.Q. ASSAM FARM (H 22 a. 2.7.)

17. Acknowledge.

[signature]

Capt. & Adjt.
for Lieut.-Col
Comdg. 17th The Royal
Scots

Issued by runner at

Copy No.1 O.C. W Coy
    2 " X "
    3 " Y "
    4 " Z "
    5 106 Bde. H.Q.
    6 12th H.L.I.
    7 18th H.L.I.
    8 T.O. and Q.M.
    9 M.O.
   10 2nd in Command
   11 Signal Officer
   12 Intelligence
   13 War Diary
   14 & 15 O.C. File.

Army Form C. 2118.

WAR DIARY
INTELLIGENCE SUMMARY.

17th (S) Bn. The Royal Scots.

Instructions regarding War Diaries and Intelligence Summaries are contained in F. S. Regs., Part II. and the Staff Manual respectively. Title pages will be prepared in manuscript. Ref. Map. 1/40,000 Sheet 28 & 29. (Erase heading not required.)

Place	Date	Hour	Summary of Events and Information	Remarks and references to Appendices
Belgian Battery Corner	Oct. 1918. 3/4th.		Battalion moved to Reserve Billets at Belgian Battery Corner. Re-organization, Equipping and Interior Economy carried out.	
V.24.a. V.20.b.	7th 11/13 14/28		Battalion moved to Brigade Reserve positions in V.24.a. Battalion moved from Brigade Reserve to Divisional Reserve in V.20.b. Battalion engaged in Active Operations in the following Areas:- GULLEGHEM, PISSEGHEM, MARCKE, to Ridge running through 0.26.d. and 0.27.c. and b. Special Report on Operations attached.	
	21st.		41st Division passed through Division, and Battalion came back to billet in vicinity of COURTRAI.	
	21/24 24th. 26th.		Battalion in rest in billets in COURTRAI. Battalion left COURTRAI and proceeded to billets in SWEVEGHEM. Bn.H.Q. at O.1.a.55. Left SWEVEGHEM at 20.00 and proceeded to take over the line in front of AVELGHEM, relieving one Coy. 15th HANTS., and one Batt. E. SURREYS. of 42nd Division. Relief complete 03.05. hours 27th. Bn.H.Q. being at P.31.a.5.5.	
	31st 31/1st		Two Coys. attacked in conjunction with 104th Brigade. Relieved by K.R.R. and proceeded to billets in N.18. area. Bn.H.Q. N.17.b.7.6.	

Battalion Strength on 1st October 1918. Offs. 23 O.R's. 573
Battalion Strength on 31st October 1918. Offs. 29 O.R's. 645

Reinforcements Offs. Lieut. H.R.Harvey 8:10:18   O.R's. 2 O.R's. 12th Oct. 1918.
             " G.E.Curry   6:10:18   79 " 16th " "
             " W.Jamieson 6:10:18   21 " 24th " "
         2/" R. Stewart, D.C.M. 15:10:18
            Lieut. D. Gellatly 24:10:18
         2/"   J.R.Cowan 24:10:18
         2/"   J.D.Crawford 30:10:18

Army Form C. 2118.

WAR DIARY

17th.(S).Bn. The Royal Scots.

Instructions regarding War Diaries and Intelligence Summaries are contained in F. S. Regs., Part II. and the Staff Manual respectively. Title pages will be prepared in manuscript.

(Erase heading not required.)

Place	Date	Hour	Summary of Events and Information	Remarks and references to Appendices

Casualties.

```
         Lieut. H.R. Harvey - W. in A. -16-10-18
              R.A. Wyllie - Classified Neurasthenia -20-10-18
   1 O.R. W.in A. 2-10-18        1 O.R.    W. in A. - 24-10-18
   2  "       "   4-10-18        1  "        "    "  - 27-10-18
   6  "       "   6-10-18        1  "      K. in A. - 31-10-18
   1  "       "   7-10-18        1  "      W. in A. - 29-10-18
   3  "       "  14-10-18        2  "       "    "  - 30-10-18
   3  "       "  18-10-18        8  "       "    "  - 31-10-18
   1  "    K.in A 18-10-18
   2  "    W.in A.17-10-18
   3  "       "  19-10-18
```

Honours and Awards.

```
   Lieut. D.M.Weatherstene,        Awarded The Military Cross.   23rd Oct. 1918.
   2/  "  H. Jarvis                    "     "     "      "       31st   "    "
       "  R.A.Wylie                    "     "     "   Medal      21st   "    "
   21937 Pte. G.W.Graham               "     "     "     "          "    "    "
   25579  "   M. Monamee                "    "     "     "          "    "    "
   29973  "   W. Milne                  "    "     "     "          "    "    "
   40511  "   W.H. Cork                 "    "     "     "          "    "    "
   35124 Cpl. H. C. Clarke              "    "    D. C. Medal      23rd  "    "
   23784 Sgt. A. White                  "    "     "     "           "   "    "
   12033 Cpl. C. Pritchard              "    "    Military Medal     "   "    "
   23554 L/Cp A. Nicol                  "    "     "        "        "   "    "
```

Ian Gordon Major.
A/Comdg. 17th (S) Bn. The Royal Scots.

17th.(S). Bn. The Royal Scots.

REPORT ON OPERATIONS engaged in by the Battalion from 13th. Oct. to 21st. Oct. 1918.

Reference Sheets 28 and 29 1/40,000

13-10-18
16.30 hours.
    The Battalion moved from Camp at GHELUVELT into assembly positions in Divisional Reserve in area K.20.a.5.8. arriving there at 19.30 hours. The Battalion remained in assembly until Zero hour.

14-10-18
05.30 hours.
    Zero hour for the attack by 104th. and 105th. Infantry Brigades. The Battalion Stood To in assembly position. Previous to Zero Brigade H.Q. moved foward and at Zero 12th. High. L.I. moved foward and occupied Front Line. At 09.15 orders were received that when the Brigade moved to Second positions of assembly 18th. High. L.I. would be on the right 17th. Royal Scots on the left (the former in L.20 c and the latter in L.26 a.)

13.10 hours.
    Orders to move to Second Assembly Positions in depth - 18th. High. L.I. to L.20 c and 17th. Royal Scots to L.19½ c

15.25 hours.
    The Battalion arrived in Second assembly position 18th. High. L.I. having moved to L.20 c and 12th. High. L.I. to L.26. Battalion H.Q. were established at WOODBINE Farm. Liason was established with the foward Battalions.

18.25 hours.
    Under orders from Brigade "A" and "C" Coys. 35th. M.G. Battalion reported to me to be under my command.

15-10-18
    The Battalion remained in its present position. At 14.00 a warning order was received that the Brigade would advance or take over the line from 104th. and 105th. Infantry Brigades. Arrangements for relief were accordingly made with O.C.18th. Lancashire Fusiliers.

22.30 hours
These were altered at Brigade conference when 12th. High. L.I and 18th. High. L.I. were ordered to attack from M.32 and M.27 27 and occupy the line of the river LYS. 17th. Royal Scots were to be in support. Zero hour was fixed at 05.30, 16-10-18 and the Battalion was ordered to assemble in area G.25 a.

16-10-18.
03.50 hours.
    Battalion assembled without incident in G.25 a. Bn. H.Q. at DERISION FARM (G.30 b.7.8). Attack commenced under Artillery barrage at 05.30. Having obtained liaison with attacking troops and as a result of favourable progress reports I decided to move to a more central and closer supp:

11.30 hours
:ort position, and shifted accordingly, to area G.28.a & b. with Battalion H.Q. in G.22 c. Close liaison was estab: lished with 12th. and 18th. High. L.I. at their joint H.Q. (G.34.c.4.7.). The Battalion remained in this location until 00.01 hours when orders were received by Telephone from Brigade that the R.E. were bridging the river and that the Battalion would cross the river LYS and occupy the Line of the Railway from M.11.b.0.9. to M.6.c.1.4.. The Battalion was assembled at the Cross Roads in BISSINGHEM (G.35.a.9.4) by 02.00 hours ready to cross. By conference it was decided

17-10-18
that the 12th. High. L.I. should provide Infantry Escorts for the bridging parties under Artillery barrage. The Bridges to be constructed were at G.36 a.5.5. - M.5.b.6.7. and M.5.c. 1.1., the two be crossed by the Battalion being at M.5 b.6.7. and M.5.c.1.1. Zero hour was arranged for 04.00 but it transpired that a barrage could not be arranged and as the bridging could not be done before daylight the operation was suspended and the Battalion returned to its reserve position.
    As a result of a Brigade Conference in the afternoon it was ordered that at 22.00 under Artillery Barrage 12th. High. L.I. with R.E. bridging parties would cross the river LYS at the bridges previously decided on and hold bridgeheads ~~bringxxxxkxbkkxxx~~ Immediately on these bridgeheads being established the Battalion was ordered to cross and hold the Line of the Railway North of MARCKE and if possible seize the village itself.

2.

I disposed the Battalion into "Z" Coy assaulting and "Y" Coy. in Support. The assault company was ordered to cross the river, seize the Railway and push foward from there into the Northern end of the village, the supporting company moving meantime to M.5 c. area in close support.

19.00 The Battalion was assembled at Cross Roads BISSINGHEM in readiness to advance to, cross the river as soon as word was received that the Bridgeheads had been established.

22.00 Bridging operations commenced. It was reported that the
23.45 Southern Bridge could not be constructed owing to enemy opposition and that the Northern Bridge could not be finished before daylight. In the centre a foot bridge had been constructed and a close bridge-head established. I therefore decided to change my plan of operations and to send a strong fighting patrol of 2 platoons across the River to work south and clear up the situation.

18-10-18 The two platoons moved off to cross the Bridge. The Officer
00.30 in charge of one of the platoons (Lieut.H.R.Harvey) was wounded almost immediately and Lieut. W.C. Inman was left in command of the party.

The patrol crossed the River without incident and operated in area M.5 b.& D. until dawn. One enemy post was rushed and the garrison xxxxxxx (3 men) captured. The other enemy posts took xx alarm and fled but about six of the enemy in all were killed or wounded by the patrol which returned xxxxxxxxxxxxxx at dawn without casualty.

05.30 The assaulting company (Z Company-Lieut. H.M.Johnstone) returned to its reserve position, and the support Company("Y" Coy. Lieut. D.M.Weatherstone) being left in area G.35 b. in support to the 12th. High. L.I. bridgehead party.

15.00. Orders were received that the Battalion would attack and capture MARCKE under an Artillery Barrage at 22.00 hours. "W" Coy. 18th. High. L.I. being attached in reserve to the Battalion. The atack was to be carried out from the West the objectives being the Canal Crossings. Railway and Esatern Exits of the Village. I disposed the Battalion for attack on a two Company front ("Z" Coy. Lieut. H.M. Johnstone) on the right and "Y" Coy.(Lieut. D.M. Weatherstone) on the left with "W" Coy. 18th. High. L.I.(Capt. Smith in Reserve.

The only approach to the assembly position was by a single plank bridge west of the Village about M.10 a.5.5.

This crossing was successfully made and the Battalion assembled to an approximate Line M.10 d.7.5. to M.10 b.5.5. by 21.3 without incident.

22.00 At Zero hour the Battalion advanced under a barrage and meeting with little opposition captured all objectives by 23.30 hou liberating in the village a large number of Civilians.

The attack was very successful, the prisoners taken amount ping to about 24 and the casualties being three men wounded. A larger number of prisoners would have been taken had not the enemy fled on our arrival. Four M.Gs were also captured.

I should liketo express my appreciation of the High L.I Coy attached who were of great value as a reserve for mopping purposes.

After reaching the objectives touch was obtained with the 12th. High. L.I. who had crossed the River and also with the Divisi on the right.

19-10-18. The Battalion remained in Posts in defence of the Village until 05.30 when troops of the 104th. Infantry Brigade passed through when the Battalion withxxxdrew into Billets in MARCKE in Divisional Reserve where it remained during the rest of the day.

20-10-18. At 02.00 ordes were received that the Brigade would march a 07.00 to EVANGELIE BOOM (N.18 central) and assemble there in close reserve to, the foward Brigades.

At 07.00 the Brigade moved off and arrived at N.9.d 3.3½/ where word was received that the Brigades infront were held up on Line N.13.- N.24. by enemy Machine Guns. At 10.00 the Battalio was ordered to move foward into area N.4 in close support to 104th and 105th. Infantry Brigades. Liaison was established by patrol with troops of these two Brigades and a report of the situation received.

The Battalion remained in this area until 16.30 hours when

orders were received to advance to KREUPEL in area O.13 c in reserve to an attack by 12th. High. L.I. and 18th. High. L.I. on objectives in O.36 and O.31.

The Battalion moved foward and assembled about N.18 where it remained in reserve. A Patrol was sent out and touch with 18th. High. L.I. obtained.

11.59

Orders were received that 18th. High. L.I. had reach:ed MOLEN TE CLAERE (O.25 d.9.1) and that the Battalion with 1 section "C" Coy. 35th. M.G. Battalion was to advance through N.19 at once and capture Line of ridge from MOLEN TE CLAERE to HOOGSTRAATJE and if possible clear down the CANAL in O.22.

21-10-18
02.00

The Battalion with attached Section M.G's moved off advanced Guard formation, 2 platoons of Z Coy. as van and main guard and Z Coy less 2 platoons and Y Coy. as main body. The plan was to advance in this formation along road through N.24 d, O.19 c & d and O.25 b. until opposition was met and then to deploy and attack the ridge frontally and occupy Line from MOLEN TE CLAERE to HOOGSTRAATJE and so couple up with 18th. High. L.I.

The advance was without incident until O.19 c.5.6. when a Very Light was fired on the line of the road and a M.G. opened. At the same time enemy M.Gs also fired from the left and right front. In order to clear the situation I halted the Battalion and sent out Lieut. W.C.Inman with two platoons to engage the M.G in front and clear the Line of advance. This patrol I covered by M.G. Fire from attached section on the suspected position of enemy Gun. (This fire, from later information, was most effective and forced the enemy to vacate his post). The Patrol returned to report all clear for 600 yards in front so in order to reach the objective before dawn I decided to push right through to the objective and mop up later any posts we had passed through. I therefore, deplo:ed the Battalion astride the road O.19 c & d and O.25 b. "Z" Coy. leading and "Y" Coy in support and advanced fight through to the objective where the leading Coy. took up a line from MOLEN TE CLAERE (O 26.c.O.O.)to O.27.c.04. HOOGSTRAATJE was found clear and an Officers Patrol was sent down to reach the CANAL but was stopped by enemy M.G. fire. By use of Vickers M.G. fire the enemy posts were driven away and the flank cleared. Meanwhile enemy posts in rear and left rear of the Battalion were heard firing and platoons were sent back to mop, as a result of which 2 prisoners were taken 1 of enemy killed and many more were seen to run away.

Liaison was established with 12th. High. L.I. on right and Line of Posts held until 21.00 when troops of another Division passed through the Battalion.

The enemy had apparently intended to defend the Canal from Frontal Attack as trench posts had been dug and a strong belt of wire erected.

The Battalion remained in position till 13.00 hours when orders were received to return to billets in N.9. & 10 which were reached by 15.00 hours.

I cannot speak too highly of the behaviour of all ranks in the Battalion. Although casualties were extraordin:arily light conditions of weather and ground were not of the best and the consequent fatigue was great. Despite being very tired and often suffering from lack of sleep all ranks were cheerful and keen and carried on without demur or complai and with undiminished enthusiasm throughout a very hard 8 day fighting.

A List of Officers and Other Ranks is being fowarded who have not only shown conspicuous gallantry but have also throughout the operations been noticeably cheerful keen and un:tiring in all their duties and so set a splendid example to all.

Jas Gordon Major
for Lieut-Col.
Comdg. 17th.(S).Bn. The Royal Sc

WAR DIARY
or
INTELLIGENCE SUMMARY.

(Erase heading not required.)

Army Form C. 2118.

Instructions regarding War Diaries and Intelligence Summaries are contained in F. S. Regs., Part II. and the Staff Manual respectively. Title pages will be prepared in manuscript.

17 R Scots

Place	Date	Hour	Summary of Events and Information	Remarks and references to Appendices
Evangelie Boom	31-10-18 to 4-11-18		In billets at Evangelie Boom, left for Courtrai on the 4-11-18.	
Courtrai	4-11-18 to 9-11-18		In billets at Courtrai marched to Ingoyghem on the 9-11-18 Training at Courtrai to Schelet crossing.	
Ingeyghem Mont de la Cruche	10-11-18 11-11-18		Left Ingeyghem and marched to Mont de la Cruche on the 10-11-18. In Bde. reserve. Left Mont de la Cruche and marched to Ten Bergg. On the march to Ten Bergg when hostilities ceased.	
Ten Bergg	to			
Eticheve	13-11-18		Left Ten Bergg and marched to Eticheve on the 13-11-18.	
Ingeyghem Staceghem	18-11-18 19-11-18		Left Eticheve and marched back to Ingeyghem on the 18-11-18. Left Ingeyghem and marched to Staceghem on the 19-11-18.	
Menin Ypres	27-11-18 28-11-18		Left Staceghem and marched to Menin on the 27-11-18. Left Menin and marched to Ypres on the 28-11-18. The Battalion marched past Princess Mary just before entering Ypres.	
Terdeghem Brexeele Moulle	29-11-18 30-11-18 1-12-18		Left Ypres and marched to Terdeghem on the 29-11-18 Left Terdeghem and marched to Brexeele on the 30-11-18. Left Brexeele and marched to Moulle on the 1-12-18.	

Lieut. Col.
Comdg. 17th (S) Bn. The Royal Scots.

17th.(S).Bn. The Royal Scots.   Army Form C. 2118.

WAR DIARY
or
INTELLIGENCE SUMMARY

DECEMBER 1918.

Reference Map 1/40,000 sheet ST.OMER.

Place	Date	Hour	Summary of Events and Information	Remarks and references to Appendices
Broxeele	Dec. 1st.			
	2nd to 6th.		Battalion moved by march route from BROXEELE to Billets in HOULLE.	
			Battalion in Billets in HOULLE. Refitting and Cleaning up generally, carried out.	
	6th.		Recreational Training and Educational Training commenced.	
	6th.		Battalion moved by march route to Camp in MERCKEGHEM, taking over Billets from Xth.Corps Gas School.	
	9th. to 17th.		Battalion moved from Gas School to Xth.Corps School Camp,vacated by the 19th.Durh.L.I. Battalion Training. Educational Training and Recreational Training carried on. FromBattalion paraded under Brigade arrangements for the presentation of Medal Ribands by the Divisional General on 15th.inst.	
	18th. to 31st.		Battalion engaged on Trench filling in Area A.33.c. and on removal of all R.E. Material, in that area. During this period Educational and Recreational Training was continued as far as possible.	

Battalion Strength. 1st.Dec.1918   → 36 Officers 774 Other Ranks.

Battalion Strength 31st.Dec.1918 — 38 Officers 701 Other Ranks.

Reinforcements.
Lieut. M.S.Kerr — To Duty from 6 mos. tour of Duty — 27-11-18.
2/Lieut. T Baird From Base   — 28-11-18.
"   J.C.Maltman   "   "   — 28-11-18.
Major C. Andersen D.S.O.M.C. From No.6 Young Officers School — 12-12-18.
2 O.Rs.   From Base. — 21-12-18.
38 O.Rs. From Base. — 25-12-18.

STRENGTH DECREASE.
2/Lieut.A. Wood   — Medical Bearded — 29-11-18.
Capt. C.A.Petherbridge M.C. — To U.K. Sick 4-12-18.
Lieut. J.B.Cameron — To Base re Demobilization — 12-12-18.
Major. A.D.Loch M.V. —   "   "   "   — 19-12-18.
Lieut. G.E.Curry   — To U.K.   "   "   — 14-12-18.
12 O.Rs. — To Base re Demobilization — 10-12-18.
18 O.Rs. —   "   "   "   — 12-12-18.
58 O.Rs. —   "   "   "   — 14-12-18.
2 O.Rs. —   "   "   "   — 30-12-18.

HONOURS AND AWARDS.
Lieut. C.P.Lancaster — French Croix de Guerre -5-12-18
29547 Sgt.H.A. Rose   —do—
271467 Pte.J.R. Piggett —do—
22400 Cpl. G.Mackintosh —do—
21909 Sgt. A.Lawrie   —do—
Lieut-Col. W.A.Murray D.S.O.M.C. M.in D.
Major. C.Anderson D.S.O.M.C. do.
Capt. C.A.Petherbridge M.C.   do.
21741 C.Q.M.S. J.Barclay   do.

Jo. Cox Major.
Comdg.17th.(S).Bn.The Royal Scots.

Army Form C. 2118

WAR DIARY

~~INTELLIGENCE SUMMARY~~

(Erase heading not required.)

Instructions regarding War Diaries and Intelligence Summaries are contained in F. S. Regs., Part II. and the Staff Manual respectively. Title Pages will be prepared in manuscript.

Place	Date	Hour	Summary of Events and Information	Remarks and references to Appendices
	3-2-19		**STRENGTH DECREASE**	
			Lieut. M.S. Kerr - To Base Demobilized - 28-1-19.	
			HONOURS AND AWARDS	
			Lieut-Col. W.A. Murray M.C. - Belgian Croix de Guerre.	
			Lieut. J. Gray - Belgian Croix de Guerre.	
			Major. J. Gordon - Military Cross.	
			5433 R.S.M. W.A. Harrison - Belgian Croix de Guerre.	
			40598. Cpl. H.C. Sykes " do	
			22450 RQMS R. Howie - Meritorious Service Medal.	
			Jas Gordon	
			Major.	
			A/Comdg. 17th.(S).Bn. The Royal Scots.	

Army Form C. 2118.

WAR DIARY

17th.(S).Bn. The Royal Scots.

Ref: Map. 1/40,000 Sheet ST.OMER.

Place	Date	Hour	Summary of Events and Information	Remarks and references to Appendices
Merckeghem	1919 Jany. 1st to 29th.		Battalion in Billets in Xth. Corps Gas School Merckeghem. Trench Filling and Salvage of R. E. Material in Area A. 23 C. carried out. Good progress in Educational and Recreational Training was also made.	
	29th.	06.00	Battalion moved on Short Notice to quell disturbance and threatening riots in Calais.	
	30th.	09.00	Battalion entrained at WATTEN for CALAIS and on arrival proceeded to Camp in No.6 Leave Camp.West. Battalion paraded under Brigade arrangements and proceeded to No. 2 Extraordinary 6 Leave Camp East, occupied by the Mutineers. The Battalion picqueted the Road running along the Eastern Band of the Camp, but no further action was necessary, the mutineers quietly leaving the Camp on being given the opportunity, and Battalion returned to No.6 Leave Camp West.	
	31st.		Brigade Route March through CALAIS.	

Battalion Strength - 1st. January 1919 = 38 Officers 701 Other Ranks.
Battalion Strength - 31st.January 1919 = 29 Officers 557 Other Ranks.

STRENGTH DECREASE

1 O.R. to Base Demobilized	- 4-1-19	5 O.Rs. to Base Demobilized	- 5-1-19
4 " " " "	- 7-1-19	8 " " " "	- 8-1-19
8 " " " "	- 9-1-19	10 " " " "	-10-1-19
13 " " " "	-11-1-19	4 " " " "	-17-1-19
11 " " " "	-18-1-19	1 " " " "	-18-1-19
9 " " " "	-19-1-19	14 " " " "	-20-1-19
13 " " " "	-21-1-19	6 " " " "	-24-1-19
1 " " " "	-25-1-19	17 " " " "	-26-1-19
12 " " " "	-27-1-19	2 " " " "	-28-1-19
2/Lieut.H.D.Ainger	- 8-1 -19	2/Lieut.J.Baird	- 9-1-19
Capt.D.M.Weatherstone M.C.	-17-1-19.	Capt.G.S.Matley	-20-1-19
Lieut.W.M.Gray	-19-1-19	Lieut.J.Gray	-21-1-19
		Lieut.P.G.Brentz M.M.	-21-1-19

Army Form C. 2118.

WAR DIARY

17th.(S).Bn.The Royal Scots.

Ref.Map. 1/40,000 Sheets St.Omer & 27 & 28

FEBRUARY 1919

Instructions regarding War Diaries and Intelligence Summaries are contained in F.S. Regs., Part II. and the Staff Manual respectively. Title pages will be prepared in manuscript.

(Erase heading not required.)

Place	Date 1919	Hour	Summary of Events and Information	Remarks and references to Appendices
Calais	Feb. 1st.		Battalion in Camp in No. 6 Leave Camp, West, Calais.	
	2nd.		Battalion returned to Merckeghem and took over Billets previously occupied in X Corps School.	
	2nd. to 8th.		Battalion in Billets in X Corps S chool. Battalion Training. Educational Training and Recreational Training carried on.	
	9th.	07.45	Battalion moved on Short notice to Calais owing to a disturbance expected with returning Leave party.	
		11.00	Battalion entrained at Watten for Calais and on arrival proceeded to Billets in Camp at Beaumairis occupied by the 2nd./23rd. London Regt.	
	11th.		No trouble arose and the Battalion returned to previous Billets in Merckeghem.	
	12th.		Battalion Training resumed.	
	20th.		Battalion was attached to Labour Groups as under for duty in patrolling and policing of the areas occupied by these Groups with a view to the stopping of the looting of trains and the protection of the B.G. Railway Line. Also to maintain proper discipline among the Chinese.	
	21st. to 28th.		Bn. H.Q............................Steenvoorde.	
			W.Company........attached 65th.Labour Group with Coy.H.Q. at J. 13 central.	BELGIUM SHEET 28.
			X.Company........attached 66th.Labour Group with Coy. H.Q. at H.23 Central.	
			Y.Company........attached 33rd. Labour Group with Coy.H.Q. at S.14.c.central.	
			Z Company........attached 32nd. Labour Group with Coy.H.Q. atB.26.c.6.4.	

Strength of Battalion on 1st. February 1919   29 Officers 557 O.Rs.
Strength of Battalion on 28th.February 1919. 27 Officers 328 O.Rs.

Strength. Decrease.

Major. J.Gordon M.C. to U.K. re Demobilization - 12-2-19
" C.Andersen D.S.O.M.C. to Base re Demob. - 15-2-19.

3.	O.Rs. to Base re Demobilization	- 3-2-19.	1	O.R. to Base re Demobilization	= 14-2-19
13	"	- 4-2-19.	34	"	= 15-2-19
5	"	- 6-2-19.	37	"	= 16-2-19
22	"	- 7-2-19.	27	"	= 19-2-19
39	"	- 8-2-19.	19	"	= 20-2-19
2	"	- 9-2-19.	1	"	= 21-2-19
1	"	- 12-2-19	5	"	= 22-2-19
3	"	- 13-2-19	1	"	= 28-2-19
1	O.R. Accidentally Killed	- 24-2-19.			

Murray. Lieut-Col.
Comdg. 17th.(S).Bn.The Royal Scots.

WAR DIARY
INTELLIGENCE SUMMARY.
(Erase heading not required.)

Army Form C. 2118.

Place	Date	Hour	Summary of Events and Information	Remarks and references to Appendices
Merchtem	1918 Oct 10th	—	Battalion, now trained to Gare, in billets in X Cafés School Merchtem.	
	11th "	—	Battalion moved to Camp at Tilques	
	18th "	—	Battalion entrained at 16.00 hours at St Omer and proceeded to Dunkirk.	
	22nd "	—	Battalion embarked at Dunkirk for Southampton	
			Strength Decrease	
			Lieut C.H. Jarvis MC. attack 365 length pending Demob. 18.12.18 § auth. G.R.C. 5974	
			2/Lieut J.L. Fair " " " " " " 23.12.18 "	

W. Murray. Lieut-Col
Comdg. 17th (S) Bn. The R. Scots.